TRETYAKOV GALLERY

GUIDE

THE TRETYAKOV GALLERY

Guide

Second edition

Editor in chief *Valentin Rodionov*,
Director General of the State Tretyakov Gallery

Selection and text by *Valentin Rodionov* ("Pages of the Gallery History"),
Galina Andreyeva and *Olga Yushkova*, with participation of *Irina Leytes*

English translation by *Julia Redkina*

Financial support of the publication by the Surgutneftegas joint-stock company

Designer *Denis Lazarev*
Photographs by *Nikolay Alexeyev, Anatoly Sapronenkov, Vitaly Nefyodov,
Igor Kozlov, Alexander Viktorov* and *Vladimir Voronov*

Editor *Irina Gutt*
Assistant editor *Natalia Tolstaya*
Proofreader *Svetlana Moseychuk*

ISBN 5-93893-171-1

P-2 Art Publishers. 11 Zvenigorodskaya St, 191119, St Petersburg, Russia
Ivan Fiodorov Printing Company, St Petersburg. 4,000 copies (6261)

PRINTED AND BOUND IN RUSSIA

Moscow enjoys the reputation of a generous and hospitable city as well as a city of energetic and practical people. The acquaintance with the Russian capital would be incomplete without a visit to the Tretyakov Gallery, the first gallery of national art opened in 1856. Preserved in this treasury of art, together with the works of famous Russian painters and sculptors, is the spirit of its early history and the traditions established by its founder Pavel Tretyakov, a merchant and philanthropist, who was an outstanding art connoisseur yet very modest man.

The gallery which will celebrate its 150th anniversary in 2006 has the vitality of youth and goes on developing through time and in space. When Pavel Tretyakov presented his collection to the city of Moscow in 1892, it numbered about 2, 000 paintings, sculptures and graphic works. Today, the gallery holds more than 130, 000 items. Its exhibition area has been extended several times. The main building is located in quiet Lavrushinsky Lane in Zamoskvorechye, Moscow's historical centre, where it used to be in Tretyakov's lifetime, while the exhibition of 20th-century art is mounted in a new building on Krymsky Val, next to the Central House (Club) of Artists where contemporary artistic life is concentrated. Several branches of the gallery have been opened, these are the Museum Church of St Nicholas in Tolmachi, the house-museum of the painter Pavel Korin, the memorial studio of the sculptor Anna Golubkina, the house-museum of Victor Vasnetsov and the memorial flat of Apollinary Vasnetsov.

The Tretyakov Gallery has always been democratic. Adhering to the best traditions of the past, it was, nevertheless, opened for innovations. Responsive to the love of the public, the gallery made its treasures available to the broad masses of the people. Its policy remains quite the same nowadays. In 1977 Georgy Kostaki's collection of Russian avant-garde art that had not been rehabilitated yet was donated to the museum, in 2001 the gallery received a collection representing the latest artistic trends and movements and in the spring of 2000 it was the first to open an exposition covering the evolution of 20th-century art which had hardly become history.

As the gallery director, I am proud of the past and present of our remarkable museum and happy to welcome everybody who comes to visit this great and somewhat "sacred" place.

Valentin Rodionov,
Director General of the State Tretyakov Gallery

PAGES OF THE GALLERY HISTORY

The State Tretyakov Gallery possesses the finest collection of Russian art in the world. Like the Hermitage and the Mariinsky Theatre in St Petersburg as well as the Kremlin and the Bolshoy in Moscow, it is regarded as a symbol of national culture.

The gallery founder, Moscow merchant and industrialist Pavel Tretyakov (1832–1898), intended it to be solely a collection of Russian painting. The foundation date of the Tretyakov Gallery is generally reckoned to be the year of 1856 when first pictures were purchased by Tretyakov.

To trace the evolution of Russian art, he acquired works of the painters who either had already contributed much to national visual culture or were active in contemporary artistic pursuits. "I select... only what I consider necessary for a complete survey of national painting," the collector wrote, explaining his policy, in a letter to Leo Tolstoy.

Tretyakov was inspired by the idea of "creating a public repository of fine arts, accessible to all." From the very beginning he meant to bequeath his collection to the state. One of the oldest curators of the gallery recalled that he used to say: "These pictures must belong to the people," and often reminded all the staff of the gallery that they were preserving and taking care of national property.

Tretyakov's contemporaries were impressed by his native wit and fastidious taste. The painter Ivan Kramskoy, his close friend and advisor, observed that he had a flair for infallibly choosing the very best and most interesting works of art. He was greatly respected by modern artists who understood that the purchase of their pictures by Tretyakov would bring them widespread recognition. It was not by chance that the collector was trusted by the artists and allowed to see their new works in studios or exhibition halls before the official opening of their shows. He acquired pictures that attracted him often in spite of the disdain of art critics or the disapproval of censors and even contrary to his own preferences. Amassing primarily contemporary realistic paintings, he never missed an opportunity to buy canvases by artists of the 18th and first half of the 19th centuries as well as works of early Russian art as he meant his collection to be the core of a museum of national art.

In the late 1860s Tretyakov began to systematically acquire portraits of eminent Russians – "writers, composers and other cultural figures." They were to form a museum within the museum: a national portrait gallery within his gallery of national art. He was undoubtedly influenced by the theory of the leading role of outstanding figures in history

Ilya Repin (1844–1930)
Portrait of Pavel Tretyakov. 1901
Oil on canvas. 110 x 132 cm

Pavel Tretyakov with his family. Photograph. 1884

The Tretyakov house and gallery building
in Tolmachi. 1890s

Nikolay Gritsenko (1856–1900)
Main Staircase in the Tretyakov House
Watercolours and gouache on paper. 35.7 x 25.7 cm

PAGES OF THE GALLERY HISTORY

which was essential for the moral attitudes of the 19th century and gained even greater popularity after the opening of the National Portrait Gallery in London in 1856. Tretyakov who since 1860 had been regularly visiting Great Britain couldn't but see this unique gallery. In the 1870s and 1880s he commissioned portraits to leading Russian painters, thus stimulating the development of this art form in Russia. Many works by Perov, Kramskoy, Repin and Yaroshenko, even though executed not as artistic commissions for Tretyakov, were oriented toward his collection of portraits.

The history of the gallery is associated with the *Peredvizhniki* (The Wanderers), or the Society for Circulating Art Exhibitions. Founded in 1870, it united artists of realistic leanings who chose to depict events and characters from Russian everyday life as well as episodes from its history. They organized mobile exhibitions of their works in all cities and towns of the Russian Empire. Tretyakov shared the aspirations of the *Peredvizhniki* who believed that art was to serve the interests of the people and tried to bring it to Russian provinces. They found in him an ardent collector and he in them persons of identical views whom he offered both moral and financial support. It was probably due to Tretyakov's encouragement and commissions that the *Peredvizhniki* didn't betray their ideals and maintained their artistic and ideological independence. Noteworthy is the fact that some Western critic called this "group of independent artists," "painters of national lifestyle" – "the Tretyakov school." The oeuvre of the *Peredvizhniki* is most fully represented in the gallery.

Tretyakov was also attracted by the works of some talented artists who were not members of the Society for Circulating Art Exhibitions. In 1874 he acquired the Turkestan series of pictures by Vasily Vereshchagin, which increased his prestige as a leading

6 THE TRETYAKOV GALLERY

Tretyakov's letter of will sent to the Moscow city council.
31 August, 1892

Members of the Society for Circulating Art Exhibitions (*Peredvizhniki*).
Photograph. 1886

Pavel Tretyakov's exhibition. The room contains paintings
by Nikolay Gay and Mikhail Nesterov. Photograph. 1898

collector of contemporary art. Far less often did he purchase canvases by the Academy artists. Unlike most of his contemporaries, he was not fond of Ayvazovsky and opposed some innovations in the art of the 1890s, though generally he used to show interest in new ideas in painting, which made him immensely popular among the young artists of the 1880s and the 1890s. Creating a picture gallery, Tretyakov rather seldom bought works of sculpture and graphic art, most of them were added to the museum after his death.

At first his acquisitions were installed in the house of the Tretyakovs in Lavrushinsky Lane purchased by the family in the early 1850s. The growth of the collection prompted Tretyakov to add additional exhibition areas to the house. In the spring of 1874 the paintings were hung in a new two-storey building of the gallery designed by the architect Alexander Kaminsky, Tretyakov's brother-in-law. The new building consisted of two spacious halls joined to the living quarters with a passage and had a separate entrance, so that the gallery visitors could enter it directly from the street. It was not before 1881 that the gallery was opened to the general public. By the late 1880s the extended gallery building contained 14 rooms and surrounded the Tretyakov house on three sides. Soon the collection received museum status. Formally remaining a private gallery, it became available to all, irrespective of their origin and social position, the admission was free.

In 1860 Tretyakov for the first time expressed his wish to donate the collection to the city of Moscow in a letter of will addressed to his family. In August, 1892, he again declared that he intended to present his gallery, to which he had added a collection of Western European and Russian paintings inherited from his deceased brother Sergey Tretyakov, to Moscow. On the 15th (27th) September of the same year, the city council gratefully accepted the donation of the Tretyakov brothers. The collection comprised 1,287 paintings, 518 drawings and 9 sculptures by Russian masters as well as 75 paintings and 8 drawings by European artists, mostly French and German, of the second half of the 19th century. In August, 1893, the museum was opened to the general public as the Moscow Municipal Gallery of Pavel and Sergey Tretyakov, the admission was also free.

In recognition of Tretyakov's services he was made an honorary citizen of Moscow. After the royal family's visit to the Tretyakov Gallery the emperor hastened to organize

the Russian Museum of Alexander III in St Petersburg, analogous to the Moscow gallery.

Pavel Tretyakov was appointed the lifelong curator of the gallery. Until his death he kept the collection growing buying pictures not only with the money allocated by the city council but also with his own and donating them to the gallery. The catalogue of the collection compiled by its founder shortly before his death (published in 1899) contained 1,635 paintings.

According to Tretyakov's will, no changes were to be made to the collection after his death. The gallery was run by the Board of Guardians (that existed until the October revolution of 1917) elected by the city council which had to solve a delicate problem: how to develop the gallery without violating the will of Tretyakov. The first board included the famous painter Valentin Serov, the art connoisseur and collector Ilya Ostroukhov and Alexandra Botkina, Tretyakov's daughter, with whom the decision rested. In 1899 a compromise was achieved by mutual efforts, it was decided to enlarge the collection but display new acquisitions separately. The decree on the status of the Tretyakov Gallery issued by the Moscow city council in 1904 stated that the gallery was to most fully cover the evolution of Russian art, so it became evident that its collections had to be complemented with new works representing contemporary trends and movements.

In 1910–1925 the gallery accommodated the collection of Western European art which consisted of the paintings bequeathed to the gallery by the Moscow industrialist and collector Mikhail Morozov (among them canvases by Edouard Manet, Auguste Renoir, Vincent Van Gogh, Edvard Munch and others) and the works amassed by Sergey Tretyakov. In 1925 this collection was transferred to museums of Western art.

In 1913 the well-known painter and art historian Igor Grabar was appointed the gallery's guardian (in 1917–1925 he was its director). Under his guidance, the gallery was radically reorganized in 1913–1915. The pictures were rearranged in chronological order. Adherence to this principle made it possible to show the development of Russian art and single out major individual "junctures," devoting separate rooms to the oeuvre of the greatest Russian artists. The new layout helped the visitors, while strolling around the gallery, "to read the well-composed book of Russian art history."

By a decree of 1918 the gallery was nationalized and turned into a state museum, thus its status of the major repository of national art was confirmed.

The first post-revolutionary decade was marked by the process of accumulation and centralization of art treasures in state depositories. The number of exhibits in the gallery increased several times as it had absorbed some nationalized private collections (through the State Museum Fund).

The growth of the gallery was so rapid and unprecedented that in 1919 its areas were divided up into the permanent display and storerooms. In 1925 the Tsvetkov gallery, famed for its superb collection of drawings and watercolours by Russian artists of the 18th – 19th centuries, and the Ostroukhov Museum of Icons and Painting where pride of place was held by beautiful old Russian icons became branches of the Tretyakov Gallery. The holdings of the Museum of Artistic Culture brought to the gallery works by so-called "left," or avant-garde, artists. In the second half of the 1920s the branches were closed and their collections were redistributed among the gallery departments. In 1925 the gallery was enlarged by the holdings of the Rumyantsev Museum, the core of which was formed by two first-class private collections of Russian painting amassed by Fyodor Pryanishnikov and Kozma Soldatenkov in the second half of the 19th century. Most of Alexander Ivanov's pictures, including his masterpiece *The Appearance of Christ to the People* (for which a special hall was designed in 1932), came to the gallery from the Rumyantsev Museum.

In the hard time of World War II the Tretyakov Gallery exhibits were evacuated to Novosibirsk and Perm. Its building was hit by a bomb, but the damage was not severe. In 1944 before the exhibits were carried back to Moscow, it was decided to enlarge the gallery. As far back as in 1936 a two-storey building designed by Alexander Shchusev was attached to the northern side of the gallery. According to the new plan of reconstruction, another two-storey pavilion was to be erected to the south of the gallery, symmetrically related to the "Shchusev building."

However, this plan was carried out only in the 1980s when the People's Artist of the USSR Yury Korolyov was appointed the gallery director. In 1982 the government initiated a programme of the gallery's reconstruction and expansion. In accordance with the programme, the historical building of the gallery was to be preserved and included into an architectural complex with two new wings joined to its northern and southern sides. While the main building was intended for permanent display, its wings would house various services.

The Church of St Nicholas in Tolmachi also became part of the museum ensemble. Since 1997 this monument of 17th-century Russian architecture has been used as the museum's church as well as a church-museum.

The reconstruction of the gallery proceeded through several stages. The construction of the wings began in 1983, in 1985 the northern wing was finished. It included storage premises and restoration workshops. It was followed in 1989 by the southern wing, known as the "Engineering Wing" that housed exhibition rooms, a conference hall, a children's studio, computer, data and engineering services. The reconstruction of the main building started in 1986, was completed in April, 1995. Its facade designed in 1902–1904 by Victor Vasnetsov to become a symbol of the gallery and an architectural landmark of Moscow was renovated. For the work on the reconstruction project the architects Igor Vinogradsky, G. Astafyev, Boris Klimov and others and the gallery director Yury Korolyov (posthumously) were awarded the State Prize of the Russian Federation.

In 1985 the Tretyakov Gallery and the State Picture Gallery of the USSR on Krymsky Val 10 (designed in 1964 – late 1970s by Yury Sheverdyayev, Nikolay Sukoyan, Mikhail Kruglov and others) formed a single museum complex which retained the name State Tretyakov Gallery. It was then that the gallery absorbed small memorial museums that became its departments: the house-museum of the painter Pavel Korin, the memorial studio of the sculptor Anna Golubkina, the house-museum of Victor Vasnetsov and the memorial flat of Apollinary Vasnetsov, as a result of which it was given the status of a museum amalgamation. The house-museum of Natalya Goncharova and Mikhail Larionov founded in 1989 is still being organized now.

This process of amalgamation was in keeping with the conception of the gallery existing on two main sites: Lavrushinsky Lane and Krymsky Val. In May, 2000, the first in Russia comprehensive exhibition of 20th-century art was mounted in the building on Krymsky Val. It provides

Pavel Tretyakov's exhibition. Paintings by Karl Bryullov and Fyodor Bruni are hung in the room's central part. Photograph. 1898

The exhibition of 1929–1931. The room contains works by Fyodor Rokotov, Dmitry Levitsky and Fedot Shubin.

Alexander Shchusev. Project of the Tretyakov Gallery's reconstruction. Perspective view of its southern side. 1944

continuity with the exhibitions in Lavrushinsky Lane which cover the past of Russian art. For the first time the history of national art is not divided up into pre-revolutionary and Soviet periods. Radical changes took place in Russian art in the mid-1910s, before the political cataclysms of the October revolution of 1917. They were caused by the ideas and creative activities of avant-garde artists who had broken with the realistic tradition and analytical approach to reality and looked for new forms.

The last rooms in the building in Lavrushinsky Lane contain exhibitions devoted to major artistic groups and trends, active in the late 19th – early 20th centuries, and shows on individual artists, major representatives of Russian Impressionism and Symbolism – Valentin Serov, Konstantin Korovin, Mikhail Vrubel and Victor Borisov-Musatov.

Displayed in the building on Krymsky Val is the Russian art of 1910 – the early 1990s. Its first rooms accommodate paintings by Kuzma Petrov-Vodkin and members of "Jack of Diamonds" group. The works of the artists who were active before and after the revolution of 1917 are for the first time exhibited side by side, with some rooms devoted solely to shows on individual masters. Russian avant-garde art is represented in the gallery to a fairly full and varied extent (in 1977 Georgy Kostaki's excellent collection of Russian avant-garde paintings and graphic works enriched the first-class holdings of the gallery). The gallery exhibitions form a full survey of the evolution of Soviet art, or the art of Socialist Realism. Today, we know the names of those painters who were persecuted and whose pictures were banned in the 1920s and 1930s. On view are also works of "under-ground" artists from the 1950s – 1970s. The pieces representing the latest trends and movements, acquired by the gallery in 2001, are being prepared for display.

The gallery ranks among most interesting museums of the world. It is home to over 130, 000 exhibits, including 50, 000 pieces of 20th-century art. In keeping with Tretyakov's idea, the gallery contains works of practically all prominent Russian artists.

The gallery goes on developing. It is planned to set up an "artistic quarter" in Lavrushinsky Lane, with a depository of icons, available to the public, and the department of graphic art opened in the buildings of historical and architectural interest in the immediate vicinity of the gallery. A new museum structure is to be put up at the corner of Lavrushinsky Lane and Kadashevskaya Embankment and a project for the renovation of the building on Krymsky Val is being drawn. The gallery is to become the cultural centre (consisting of two parts) of the large historical district of Zamoskvorechye.

Stock of paintings in the Church of St Nicholas in Tolmachi. Photograph. 1985

Church of St Nicholas in Tolmachi after restoration

EARLY RUSSIAN ART

The Treatyakov Gallery boasts the finest in the world collection of early Russian art. Its foundation was laid out by Pavel Tretyakov who understood that a survey of the evolution of national art would be incomplete without artworks from the past. His intention was realized only after his death when, according to his will, his private collection of icons was displayed in the gallery. "A Short Description of the Icons from Pavel Tretyakov's Collection" was published in 1905. At that time no other museum in Russia had an exhibition of old icons.

A number of expositions held in Russia and abroad in 1906–1913 won the Russian icon international recognition as a greatest phenomenon of world artistic culture.

In the first decade of the 20th century there appeared a number of new private collections of early Russian art, most remarkable of them were those of Ilya Ostroukhov, Bogdan and Varvara Khanenko, Alexey Morozov and Sergey Ryabushinsky. Contemporaries recalled that when the famous French artist Matisse was in Moscow and visited the Ostroukhov museum of icons, he was stunned by their beauty. At the same time art connoisseurs and experts were deeply concerned with the preservation of Russia's artistic heritage. In 1912 Alexander Anisimov delivered a speech "On the Destiny of Old Icons in Russia" in which he offered "to examine all church storerooms, register and save everything that can be saved... and transfer it to state property..." His plan was to be carried out some time later, after a tragic twist of history, in the most complicated period following the revolution of 1917...

In the next decade the gallery collection of early Russian art was formed under the supervision of the All-Russia Commission for the Preservation of Early Russian Painting organized by Igor Grabar and renamed into the Central Restoration Workshops in 1924. In 1918 – 1920s the commission succeeded in finding and restoring a great number of 12th – 13th-century icons painted before the Mongol invasion and icons from the village of Vasilyevskoye and the town of Zvenigorod created by Andrey Rublyov and the painters of his school.

In 1929, after the death of Ostroukhov, his collection, famed for Northern and Novgorod icons, was added to the gallery stocks. One of the most interesting pieces is the so-called "Blue Dormition" dating from the 15th century, a fine specimen of the Tver school. In 1930 best icons from the holdings of the Historical Museum were transferred to the gallery. Thus the Tretyakov Gallery came to possess the collection of icons, unrivalled in its quality.

In the early 1930s the gallery, together with the Central Restoration Workshops (now, Grabar's All-Russia Artistic and Scientific Centre for Restoration), began to send expeditions to the Moscow, Volga and Arkhangelsk regions, the cities of Novgorod and Pskov. It took much time and effort to register all the icons kept in churches, most of which were closed, and the stocks of provincial museums. The icons discovered by the expeditions were taken to Moscow, restored and then either sent back to their churches and museums or displayed in the gallery. This work went on until World War II and was resumed in the late 1950s – early 1960s.

Today the collection of early Russian art keeps growing thanks to new acquisitions and gifts. Thus in 1967 the gallery received a superb selection of icons bequeathed to it by the renowned artist and restorer Pavel Korin, now it is exhibited in his house-museum which is a branch of the gallery.

The tradition of using icons (frescoes, mosaics and paintings on wood) in liturgical life came to Russia from Byzantium after its conversion to Christianity. Among the extant Byzantine works is the **Vladimir icon of the Mother of God** (1100 – 1130s),

1. Room of early Russian art

2. **The Vladimir icon of the Mother of God**. 1100–1130s. Constantinople
Tempera on panel. 104 x 69 cm

one of the most venerated icons in Russia. It was brought to the country from Constantinople in the reign of Prince Yury Dolgoruky and kept in a convent of Vyshgorod near Kiev. With the rising of the Vladimir-Suzdal principality, the icon was sent by Andrey Bogolyubsky to Vladimir, from which it took its name. During Timur's invasion of Russia in 1395, the icon was removed to Moscow where it made the enemy army, many times outnumbering the Russian troops, retreat from the walls of the city without a battle. The iconographic type of the Virgin holding the Child who is caressing her cheek is known as Eleusa ("Tenderness"). The spirituality and artistic perfection of the image and its role in the history of the country made it one of the most popular icons in Russia. Today, it is to be found in the Church of St Nicholas in Tolmachi that belongs to the Tretyakov Gallery.

There are only few works that survive from the pre-Mongolian, or Kievan, period, these include fragments of mosaics, one of which portrays **St Demetrius of Thessalonica** (1108–1113), and frescoes that once decorated the Church of the Archangel Michael in the monastery of the same name (also called Zlatoverkhy, which means "gold-domed"). The stone relief *Two Horsemen* (*c.* 1062 – early 12th century) has been found in the territory of the monastery.

The second biggest cultural centre of old Russia was Novgorod which evolved a distinctive local style. The Novgorod school is well represented in the Tretyakov Gallery which holds a number of 11th – 12th-century Novgorodian icons (in other parts of Russia icons from the period were destroyed by the Mongol invasion) that are marked by monumentality. One of them is the ***Ustyug Annunciation*** (1130s – 1140s). The name of the icon derives from the uncertified legend relating it to the town of Veliky Ustyug. The *Annunciation* once adorned St George's Cathedral in the Yuryev Monastery of Novgorod, a most imposing church structure in ancient Russia.

Many Novgorodian icons combine elements of the Byzantine and local styles (*St Nicholas with Selected Saints*, late 12th – early 13th centuries). St Nicholas, bishop of Myra in Asia

3. *St Demetrius of Thessalonica*. 1108–1113. Kiev
Mosaic. Mortar, smalt (glass), brick and stone. 214.5 x 122 cm

4. *The Ustyug Annunciation*. 1130s – 1140s. Novgorod
Tempera on panel. 238 x 168 cm

THE TRETYAKOV GALLERY

Minor who lived in the 4th century, is one of most revered saints in Russia. He is believed to protect in danger and help in business and is reputed a "miracle-worker" and "protector of Christians." He is prayed before someone embarks on a travel, either by land or sea.

The ***Image Not-Made-By-Hands of Our Lord Jesus Christ*** (second half of the 12th century) represents a similar type of icon. The *Exaltation of the Cavalry Cross* is depicted on its reverse. The image of Christ was very popular in Novgorod where it had been venerated for centuries and which had many churches dedicated to it.

According to tradition, the king Abgar of Edessa was gravely ill and wrote to Christ asking to be cured, then he sent his servant, an artist, to Jerusalem to paint a portrait of Jesus. When the Lord saw that the artist failed to do it, he took a linen cloth and wiped his wet face with it. The image of his features became imprinted on the material. The cloth could work miracles and Abgar was healed.

The **icon of the Mother of God "The Great Panagia," or the Orant** (first third of the 13th century) was painted for one of the churches in Yaroslavl, a major town in the Vladimir-Suzdal principality. Christ Immanuel is pictured in a gold halo on the breast of the Virgin. The majestic figure of Mary with her arms outspread in prayer emphasizes her role as intercessor for people.

5. **The icon of the Mother of God "The Great Panagia,"
or the Orant.** 1200–1230s. Yaroslavl
Tempera on panel. 193.2 x 120.5 cm

6. *The Image Not-Made-By-Hands of Our Lord Jesus Christ*
Second half of the 12th century. Novgorod
Tempera on panel. 77 x 71 cm

In the 13th century when the ties between Byzantium and Russia were loosened, local styles of painting assumed a new importance. In Novgorodian icons the composition was simplified, the silhouette became bold and the palette was enriched by bright colours, with characteristic cinnabar in the background (*The Prophet Elijah*, mid-15th century). Icons began to show scenes illustrating local history. *The Miracle Wrought by the Icon of the Mother of God "Of the Sign" ("The Battle Between the Men of Novgorod and the Men of Suzdal")* (mid-15th century) is based on a certain historical event. Legend records that when in 1170 the armies of several central principalities besieged Novgorod, the city was miraculously saved by the icon of the Mother of God "Of the Sign" and the Novgorodians won the battle. This image is considered the patron icon of Novgorod and is to be found in St Sophia's Cathedral, the city's main church. The composition consists of several episodes. The scene in the upper row shows the icon carried to St Sophia's Cathedral and placed atop the fortress wall, the middle scene depicts the meeting of the representatives of the conflicting sides and the men of Suzdal shooting arrows at the fortress. The lower scene shows Novgorodians led by the holy warriors, Sts George, Boris and Gleb, and completely defeating the enemy. The icon was executed shortly before the annexation of Novgorod to the principality of Moscow (1478) and expressed the patriotic feelings of Novgorodians who were eager to preserve their independence.

The cult of Sts Florus and Laurus as healers and patrons of herds was popular in the north of Russia and Novgorod. *The Miracle of the Archangel Michael and Sts Florus and Laurus* (late 15th – early 16th century) portrays the Archangel Michael giving Sts Florus and Laurus their herd of horses.

The local school of painting took shape in the Russian city of Pskov in the 13th – 14th centuries when the city developed into an important political and cultural centre. The earliest Pskov icon on display is the *Prophet Elijah in the Desert with Scenes from His Life and the Deesis* (second half of the 13th century) which demonstrates the Pskovian independent style of painting. Pskov icons are distinguished by their intense emotionalism and unique colour scheme dominated by fiery orange-red, deep olive green, dark blue and various shades of brown. In contrast to the balanced and clear compositions of the Novgorod school and the tenderness and curved lines of the Moscow and central

7. *The Miracle Wrought by the Icon of the Mother of God "Of the Sign" ("The Battle Between the Men of Novgorod and the Men of Suzdal")*. Mid-15th century. Novgorod
Tempera on panel. 133 x 99 cm

8. *The Prophet Elijah*. Mid-15th century. Novgorod
Tempera on panel. 75 x 57 cm

9. *The Miracle of the Archangel Michael and Sts Florus and Laurus*. Late 15th – early 16th century. Novgorod
Tempera on panel. 47 x 37 cm

Russian schools, the Pskov painting shows a strong rhythmic quality. The more developed Pskovian style is represented by the ***Selected Saints: Sts Parasceva, Gregory the Theologian, John Chrysostom and Basil the Great*** (15th century). ***Sts Boris and Gleb Riding Horses*** (second half of the 14th century) is most probably another work from Pskov. The subject of the composition is a miraculous vision of some prisoners who prayed to be saved and saw Sts Boris and Gleb riding horses. Boris and Gleb, first Russian saints, were sons of Prince Vladimir I who had converted Russia to Christianity. Killed by their elder brother Svyatopolk, they were canonized by the Church soon after their death as holy martyrs and were venerated as patrons of warriors and protectors of the Russian land.

The town of Tver was another political centre of old Russia. A fine specimen of the Tver school is the ***Dormition*** (15th century), known as the "Blue Dormition" due to the blue colour predominating in its refined palette. The composition shows the deathbed of the Virgin, Christ receiving into his arms the soul of his Mother in the form of a swaddled baby, apostles, holy bishops and angels carrying the apostles on the clouds. Depicted at the top of the icon is the assumption of Mary and the episode of handing her belt to the apostle Thomas who was late for the Dormition.

Most of the ecclesiastical artists remained anonymous, only few names of outstanding icon painters have come down to the present. In 1325 the metropolitan seat was transferred from Vladimir to Moscow, thereafter the latter was to become the chief political and ecclesiastical centre in the north-east of Russia. The flowering of the Moscow school occurred under the influence of the Byzantine painter **Theophanes the Greek** (mid-14th century – after 1405). The main source of information on his life is a letter of the mediaeval writer Epiphanius the Wise, he is also mentioned in chronicles. The painter's early career was spent in Constantinople and Kefe (Feodosiya) in the Crimea, later he moved to Russia. Epiphanius names three cities where Theophanes worked: Novgorod, Nizhny Novgorod and Moscow.

10. ***The Prophet Elijah in the Desert with Scenes from His Life and the Deesis***
Second half of the 13th century. Pskov
Tempera on panel. 141 x 111 cm

11. ***Selected Saints: Sts Parasceva, Gregory the Theologian, John Chrysostom and Basil the Great.*** 15th century. Pskov
Tempera on panel. 147 x 134 cm

12. ***Sts Boris and Gleb Riding Horses***
Second half of the 14th century. Pskov
Tempera on panel. 128 x 67.5 cm

He was a representative of the new theological movement of monastic ascetics (hesychasm) and new iconographic tradition corresponding to it.

Practitioners of hesychasm seek divine quietness and purity through the contemplation of God in uninterrupted ("pure") prayer and believe that human eyes may become able to see the uncreated light, or energy, that once appeared during Christ's transfiguration.

The acquisition of the Holy Spirit involves the whole human being – the soul, mind and body and the deification of man transfigures all of them. One of the artworks inspired by this teaching is the *Transfiguration* (1403?). Jesus took the apostles Peter, John and James up Mt Tabor. There he transfigured before them, his face shone like the sun and his clothes became as white as the light. Christ is standing on the mountain, emitting the divine light. The prophets Moses and Elijah are placed on either side of him. Depicted below are the apostles who have fallen prostrate before the vision. The traditional composition has two additional scenes: Christ ascending and descending the mountain with his disciples. In the upper corners of the icon there are the figures of angels carrying the prophets to the mountain. The light is interpreted as divine energy transfiguring human flesh.

The **Don icon of the Mother of God** (1380s – 1390s) is also ascribed to Theophanes the Greek. Its reverse side contains the *Dormition* scene (1390s). The icon comes from the Dormition Cathedral in the town of Kolomna which was built to commemorate the greatest battle of Dimitry Donskoy with the Tartars on the field of Kulikovo.

Frescoes in the Annunciation Cathedral of the Moscow Kremlin (1405, non-extant) were painted by Theophanes with the assistance of another brilliant master of early Russian art **Andrey Rublyov** (*c.* 1360/ 1370 – 1430s). Very little is known of his life. Chronicles say that he was a monk. There is evidence that he worked with Daniil Chorny on the frescoes of the Dormition Cathedral in Vladimir in 1408 and, again with Chorny, was engaged in the decoration of the newly-built cathedral in the Trinity-St Sergius Monastery in 1424–1425 (the paintings were destroyed in the 17th century). After that the artists who were monks of the St Andronicus Monastery in Moscow returned home.

The *Trinity* (1420s), Rublyov's most famous icon and greatest masterpiece of Russian art, was done for the Trinity-St Sergius Monastery.

13. *The Dormition.* 15th century. Tver
Tempera on panel. 113 x 88 cm

14. Theophanes the Greek (?). Mid-14th century – after 1405
The Don icon of the Mother of God. 1380s – 1390s. Moscow
Tempera on panel. 86 x 67 cm

15. Master of Theophanes the Greek's circle
The Transfiguration. Early 15th century (1403?). Moscow
Tempera on panel. 184 x 134 cm

Rublyov produced this icon in memory of St Sergius of Radonezh, the founder of the monastery and one of Russia's most respected spiritual leaders. St Sergius called for the country's religious renewal and took tremendous efforts to unite the scattered Russian principalities.

The Biblical subject of the appearance of three angels to the patriarch Abraham and his wife Sarah (known in Russian art as the Old Testament Trinity) is regarded by theologians as a symbol of the Christian doctrine of the Trinity: that God is of one nature, yet three persons. There exist different interpretations of the icon. According to one of them, the angel in the middle represents Christ (he wears Jesus' traditional clothes), the left one God the Father and the right one the Holy Spirit. The artist's contemporaries might see in this work the embodiment of their ideal of the "perfect world," the harmonious world of Christian love and unanimity preached by St Sergius. Three other icons by Rublyov – the **Saviour**, the **Archangel Michael** and the **Apostle Paul** come from the town of Zvenigorod.

In the reign of Ivan III the principalities of Yaroslavl (1463), Rostov (1474) and Tver (1485) and the republic of Novgorod (1477) were annexed to Moscow which became the capital of the new centralized state. In 1453 the Byzantine empire collapsed and in 1480 Russia was liberated from the Mongol yoke which had lasted for two hundred and fifty years. The young Muscovite state acquired the consciousness of being the last bulwark of Eastern Orthodoxy. It was then that claims were put that Moscow would become the "third Rome" (in succession to Constantinople and Rome itself). The rise of Moscow was accompanied by a flourishing of its art and culture.

16. Andrey Rublyov (c. 1360/1370 – 1430s)
The Archangel Michael (from the town of Zvenigorod)
Early 15th century. Moscow. Tempera on panel. 158 x 106 cm

17. Andrey Rublyov (c. 1360/1370 – 1430s)
The Saviour (from the town of Zvenigorod). Early 15th century
Moscow. Tempera on panel. 158 x 106 cm

18. Andrey Rublyov (c. 1360/1370 – 1430s)
The Apostle Paul (from the town of Zvenigorod). Early 15th century
Moscow. Tempera on panel. 160 x 109 cm

19. Andrey Rublyov
(*c.* 1360/1370 – 1430s)
The Trinity. 1420s. Moscow
Tempera on panel. 142 x 114 cm

20. Dionysius
(late 1430s – after 1504)
Metropolitan Alexius with Scenes from His Life. 1480s
Moscow. Tempera on panel.
197 x 152 cm

Sculpture was far less popular in old Russia than icon painting. Most of the extant pieces were created either in the north of the country, the Urals or Siberia. A rare example of Moscow's white-stone statuary is ***St George*** (1464). The sculpture of St George, hailed the patron saint of Moscow, was executed by **Vasily Yermolin** (? – 1481/1485) for the Frolovskiye (or Saviour) gate of the Moscow Kremlin.

The most distinguished artistic personality of the Moscow school in the second half of the 15th century was Dionysius (late 1430s – after 1504). In 1482 he was entrusted with restoring the famous Greek icon of the Mother of God Hodegetria destroyed by a fire in the Ascension Monastery of the Kremlin. In his mature years he worked in the Beloozersk province (north of Russia). In 1500 he painted a number of icons for the Monastery of St Paul of Obnorsk, two of which are exhibited in the Tretyakov Gallery – the ***Saviour in Glory*** and the ***Crucifixion.*** The complex of frescoes in the St Therapont Monastery of the Nativity of the Mother of God is a genuine masterwork created by Dionysius, together with his sons Feodosy and Vladimir, in 1500–1502. The oeuvre of Dionysius reveals his ideal of ascetic monastic cenobitic life which should combine the quest for spiritual perfection with a pious disciplined life. This ideal is personified by ***Metropolitan Alexius with Scenes from His Life*** (1480s), who was a prominent church leader and a holy man. Dionysius' icons have a solemn contemplative quality, his colours are subtle and pure. It was by no chance that his refined manner was conducive to the formation of the Moscow school of painting in the late 15th – early 16th centuries.

21. *"Blessed are the Hosts of the Heavenly King" (The Militant Church)*. 1550s. Moscow
Tempera on panel. 144 x 396 cm

22. *The Appearance of the Archangel Michael to Joshua, Son of Nun (Sapega's banner).* Early 17th century
Embroidery of the Stroganov school
Fabric, silk and metallic threads. 165.5 x 180.5 cm

23. Vasily Yermolin (? – 1481/1485)
St George. 1464. Moscow
Fragment of the sculpture. Tempera on limestone

The council of 1551 formulated main principles of icon painting. It was not prohibited to show historical events along with ecclesiastical subjects. Thus, in the 1550s, a rare icon, ***"Blessed are the Hosts of the Heavenly King" (The Militant Church)*** was created to commemorate the conquest of the Kazan khanate by Ivan IV (Ivan the Terrible) in 1552, as a result of which vast territories up to the Caspian Sea were annexed to Moscow. The icon depicts an army moving from a fortress (Kazan) devoured by flames towards the Heavenly Jerusalem (Moscow). The army is led by the Archangel Michael, the "supreme commander of the heavenly hosts," represented in a fiery circle. He is followed by Ivan IV and Prince Vladimir who converted Russia to Christianity. The icon is full of symbolical implications. There are allegorical parallels between the heavenly hosts and Russian troops, the first Russian tsar and the Heavenly King. It is a pictorial paean to the victorious Christian state and the powerful Russian monarchy that had inherited the grandeur and glory of Byzantium and Rome.

The art of the Russian north was stylistically diverse and independent of other schools. Its main trend arising in the 16th – 17th centuries came to be called the Stroganov school after the wealthy family of Stroganov who succeeded in employing best masters, primarily those who worked for the tsar at the State Armoury, in their northern domain in Solvychegodsk. In the 16th century the town turned into a major artistic centre of the Russian north. The Stroganovs contributed much to the development

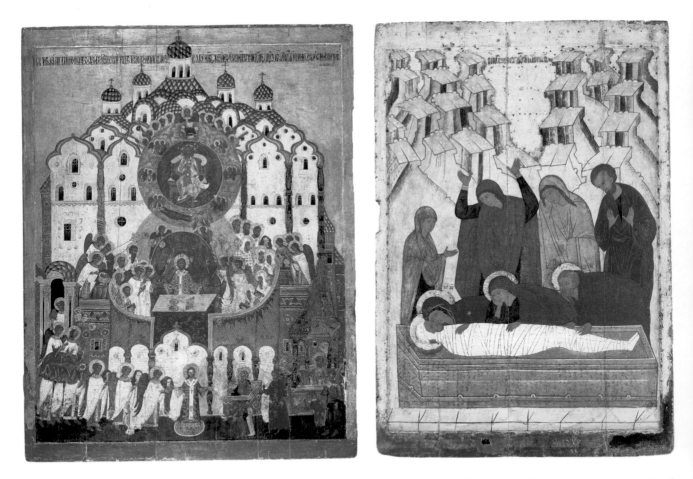

of gold embroidery (church covers, veils and shrouds), chasing and filigree work. In the late 17th century a unique local school of enamel work emerged in the town of Usolye.

"Let Us Who Mystically Represent the Cherubim" (second half of the 16th century) commissioned by the Stroganovs illustrates the Cherubim Hymn sung during the Liturgy of John Chrysostom. The portrayal of real people (members of the Stroganov family praying in the church) is an innovation. In the late 16th – 17th centuries the Stroganov school displayed both the decorativeness of folk art and the sophistication of European painting which the artists of the school were undoubtedly acquainted with. Most illustrious representatives of this trend were Prokopy Chirin, Istoma Savvin and his sons, Nazary and Nikifor.

Solvychegodsk icons were mostly designed for private use and are characterized by their miniature technique and exquisite refinement of detail. They often portrayed patron saints of the Stroganov family as well as saints revered in the north. The *Solovki Monastery of Sts Zosimas and Sabbatius* (early 17th century) represents famous Christian ascetics, founders of the largest and most important monastery in the north.

The 17th century was an eventful but rather unfavourable period for Russian icon painting when the major artistic activity was shifting to secular art. The leading master of the 17th century was **Simon Ushakov** (1626–1686) who directed the Armoury in Moscow, the country's chief artistic centre, for more than twenty years. One of his most interesting pieces is the *Tree of the State of Muscovy* (1668) which has as its model representations of Jesus' genealogy. The painting shows Prince Ivan Kalita and metropolitan Peter planting a grapevine, a symbol of sanctity, at the foundation of the Dormition Cathedral in the Moscow Kremlin. The branchy stem supports the Vladimir icon of the Mother of God, the patron icon of Moscow. Placed around it in medallions are the portraits of Moscow princes and tsars and bishops of the Russian Church.

24. *"Let Us Who Mystically Represent the Cherubim"*
Second half of the 16th century. Solvychegodsk
Tempera on panel. 197 x 153 cm

25. *The Entombment.* Last quarter of the 15th century. Central Russia
Tempera on panel. 91 x 63 cm

26. *St George Slaying the Dragon.* First quarter of the 16th century
Central Russia. Tempera on panel. 115 x 98 cm

All of them hold scrolls containing words from the Akathist (long hymn) to the Mother of God. At the bottom, outside the Kremlin walls, tsar Alexey Mikhailovich, with his wife and sons, pray to the Virgin asking her for intercession. Sensitive to the changes in contemporary art, Ushakov created the icon that expressed the patriotic aspirations of his time which supported the Orthodox monarchy regarding it as both secular and religious authority. He promoted the development of secular art, executing portraits of the royal family and making drawings for book illustrations. He also was the first to employ linear perspective.

Nikita Pavlovets (?–1677) was Ushakov's contemporary whose manner is distinguished by minuteness of detail. His **icon of the Mother of God "The Garden Close-Locked"** (c. 1670), a genuine masterpiece, reveals sincere religious feelings. While painting the icon with calligraphic precision, the artist used subtle colours to convey the unearthly beauty of the marvelous garden of the Virgin resplendent with delicate flowers.

In the 17th century there appeared first *parsunas* (a distorted form of "person"), the forerunners of secular portraits. Likenesses of prominent people were painted in tempera on panel and looked very much like icons. An example of this is *Prince Mikhail Skopin-Shuysky* (c. 1630?). The new art form gradually acquired characteristics of European secular portrait and *parsunas* began to be painted in oil on canvas. Their influence continued to be felt much later, in 18th-century portraits. Even after Peter I's reforms, early Russian art had important significance for the evolution of national visual culture. Traditional icons were produced along with those done in a more secular style.

27. Simon Ushakov (1626–1686)
The Tree of the State of Muscovy. 1668
Tempera on panel. 105 x 62 cm

28. Nikita Pavlovets (?–1677)
The icon of the Mother of God
"The Garden Close-Locked." C. 1670
Tempera on panel. 33 x 29 cm

29. *Prince Mikhail Skopin-Shuysky* (*parsuna*). C. 1630 (?)
By icon painters of the royal workshop
Tempera on panel. 41 x 33 cm

30. **Icon of the Mother of God Hodegetria. Frame:** Late 13th – early 14th centuries. Byzantium
Gilded and chased silver. 40 x 32 cm

Treasury

31. Icon containing relics: **St John the Baptist, the Angel of the Desert**
Late 17th century. Moscow. Tempera on panel, leukos (gesso white ground)
Frame: late 17th century. Moscow
Silver 800 and coloured glass; filigree and coloured enamel. 11 x 9 cm

32. **Tabernacle**. 1912. Moscow
Gilded, chased and engraved silver 875; filigree, granulation
and champlevé enamel. 60 x 27.6 x 27.6 cm

33. Anonymous artist
Miniature: **Portrait of Countess Yekaterina Shuvalova**. 1787
Medallion. Bone, gold, strass stones
and watercolour. 3.6 x 2.8 cm

The **Treasury** contains the better part of the gallery collection of objects fashioned of precious stones and metals. Its rooms hold early Russian icons and icons from later periods mounted in gold and gilded silver, pieces of exquisite gold and silver embroidery ornamented with pearls and gems (they were produced by talented Russian seamstresses both in nunneries and royal palaces), specimens of artistic forgery, bone and wood carving and jewellery from the 12th to the early 20th centuries. Noteworthy are the miniatures by 18th – early 20th-century Russian and Western painters in precious frames and church books decorated with silver and coloured stones.

The art of jewellery had evolved in Russia long before its conversion to Christianity. Its techniques, forms and motifs reflected ancient local styles, pagan cults and traditions of the tribes living near the Slavs: Scyths, Ugrians, Finns and Scandinavians as well as the influence of the artistic cultures of Asia, the East and the West.

Though Russian gold- and silverwork kept developing, it mostly employed traditional methods and techniques. In the late 19th century many workshops produced splendid jewellery and objects of decorative art, alongside the renowned firm of Faberge. On display are superb objects of luxury made by Fyodor Mishukov and Dmitry Shelaputin.

RUSSIAN ART IN THE 18TH – FIRST HALF OF THE 19TH CENTURIES

The 18th century was a time of drastic change in Russia. The abolition of the patriarchate in 1703 and other reforms of Peter I led to the secularization of social and cultural life. Russian art shifted away from its hitherto almost exclusively religious nature and became quite secular in character and oriented towards rich and varied European traditions. Peter I enlisted a great number of masters from foreign countries not only to work in Russia but train Russian artists. He introduced a system of "pensioners," gifted young men who were educated abroad at public expense. First comprehensive royal and private collections of European art were amassed.

The Academy of Art, the most significant artistic institution, was opened in the mid-18th century where leading historical and landscape painters were trained. However, the greatest achievements in 18th-century art came in portraiture. Most of its representatives started their careers as icon painters. The age-old tradition of icon painting not only influenced the artistic idiom of the new art form but infused it with deep spirituality and psychological profundity.

In the late 18th – early 19th centuries Russia was involved in military campaigns both in the East and in the West. Competing with Britain which had great sea power, Russia gained a strategically important outlet to the Black Sea. It also played a decisive role in the defeat of Napoleon. The entry of the Russian troops into Paris in 1814 was regarded by Europeans as Russia's triumph and Emperor Alexander I was called the "liberator of Europe."

These historical events stirred the imagination of the contemporaries and couldn't but influence their attitudes. The educated elité was inspired by the Romantic ideal. Declaring "noble impulses of the spirit" its main values, Romanticism was preoccupied with the hero, a free, noble, often passionate personality, deserving to be imitated. The art of portraiture reached its zenith. The Romantic cult of beauty and poetry strove to improve and ennoble "imperfect" human nature, the lifestyle of man and the scenery around him. The lofty moral and aesthetic ideal of Romanticism found its expression in genres, other than portraiture: historical painting (*The Appearance of Christ to the People* by Alexander Ivanov) and everyday scenes (*The Major's Marriage Proposal* by Pavel Fedotov).

The art of Peter I's era of reforms attained a secular character, yet retained some traces of the early tradition. Thus, in the mid-17th – first half of the 18th centuries the techniques and methods of icon painting were applied to the new art form of *parsuna*-portraits. This can be seen in the **Portrait of Tsar Mikhail Fyodorovich Romanov**, the first tsar in the Romanov dynasty (1728, copy of the 1636 original), painted by **Johann Wedekind** (1674–1736).

34. Suite of rooms containing 18th-century paintings

35. Johann Wedekind (1674–1736)
Portrait of Tsar Mikhail Fyodorovich Romanov. 1728
Oil on canvas. 204.5 x 108.3 cm

Ivan Nikitin (*c.* 1680 – after 1742) was one of the first Russian portrait painters. After studying art in Italy, he demonstrated a high level of professionalism. The ***Portrait of Count Gavriil Golovkin*** (1720s) gives an example of his work at his mature best. Golovkin, Peter I's associate, was the state chancellor, senator and head of the foreign ministry.

Foreign artists who came to work in Russia actively promoted the development of national art in the first half of the 18th century. The refined style of French painting is manifested in the likeness of Peter I's grandchildren, the ***Portrait of Tsarevich Peter Alexeyevich and Tsarevna Natalya Alexeyevna as Apollo and Diana in Their Childhood*** (1722?) by **Louis Caravaque** (1684–1754).

36. Ivan Nikitin (*c.* 1680 – after 1742)
Portrait of Count Gavriil Golovkin. 1720s
Oil on canvas. 90.9 x 73.4 cm

37. Louis Caravaque (1684–1754)
Portrait of Tsarevich Peter Alexeyevich
and Tsarevna Natalya Alexeyevna as Apollo
and Diana in Their Childhood. 1722 (?)
Oil on canvas. 94 x 118 cm

38. Georg Grooth (1716–1749)
Equestrian Portrait of Empress Elizabeth Petrovna
with a Negro Servant. 1743
Oil on canvas. 85 x 58.5 cm

The artist from France lived in Russia for over thirty five years and contributed much to its culture. He worked as an interior decorator, designed decorations for the coronation and clothes for Empress Anna Ioannovna (he was her court painter) and painted portraits. Caravaque's most talented Russian disciple was Ivan Vishnyakov (1699–1761). The expressive colours and fragile forms of his *Portrait of Prince Fyodor Golitsin* (1760) betray the influence of his French teacher. The rigid immobile posture of the sitter and the flatness of his figure indicate the portrait's stylistic similarity to the *parsuna* tradition.

Georg Grooth (1716–1749) was one of most remarkable German painters working in St Petersburg. His ***Equestrian Portrait of Empress Elizabeth Petrovna with a Negro Servant*** (1743) is a fine sample of small-size portraiture. Its decorativeness, saturated colours and elegant composition made the picture very popular with the public. The Meissen factory produced a great number of porcelain figurines modelled on the painting.

Celebrating the Marriage Contract (1777) by **Mikhail Shibanov** (? – after 1789) is a rare example of 18th-century genre scene. The large size of the canvas, its composition and techniques have much in common with historical paintings. The artist deserves credit for the faithful representation of the lifestyle of Suzdal peasants. Their dress, headgear and embroidery are rendered with precision.

The Academy of Art founded in St Petersburg in 1757 had a powerful impact on local art. Historical painting was con-

sidered most important by the Academy. Its leading exponent was **Anton Losenko** (1737–1773). ***Hector's Farewell to Andromache*** (1773) was his last and best composition, a fine example of Russian Classicism. The sketch for the picture, executed with greater freedom and dynamism, is close to the Baroque style.

The national school of art was formed in the mid-18th century. An illustrious artist of the period was Alexey Antropov (1716–1795). His *Portrait of the Lady-in-Waiting Anastasiya Izmaylova* (1759)

39. Fyodor Rokotov (1735(?)–1808)
Portrait of an Unknown Lady in Rose. Early 1770s
Oil on canvas. 58.8 x 46.7 cm

40. Anton Losenko (1737–1773)
Hector's Farewell to Andromache. 1773
Oil on canvas. 155.8 x 211.5 cm

41. Mikhail Shibanov (? – after 1789)
Celebrating the Marriage Contract. 1777
Oil on canvas. 199 x 244 cm

42. Ivan Argunov (1729–1802)
Portrait of an Unknown Woman in Russian Peasant Dress. 1784
Oil on canvas. 67 x 53.6 cm

demonstrates a powerful expressiveness of bright colours, precise characterization of the model and meticulous rendering of detail.

The late 18th – early 19th century was the heyday of Russian sculpture. The brilliant masters Fedot Shubin, Fyodor Gordeyev, Mikhail Kozlovsky, Feodosy Shchedrin, Ivan Prokofyev and Ivan Martos, who designed the famous monument to Minin and Pozharsky in Red Square in Moscow, were active in the period.

The Tretyakov Gallery houses an excellent collection of **Fedot Shubin's** (1740–1805) sculptures. Born in the Russian north, in the village of Kholmogory, famed for its bone carving, he enjoyed the patronage of Mikhail Lomonosov, a celebrated scientist and the founder of the Russian Academy of Science, who came from the same parts. Having graduated from the St Petersburg Academy of Art, Shubin went to Italy and France. He was the most prominent master of sculptural portraits. Among his sitters were members of influential aristocratic families: the Orlovs, Chernyshyovs and Golitsins. He masterfully conveyed individual characteristics of his models and had a perfect command of sculptural techniques. Pride of place belongs to his ***Portrait of Prince Alexander Golitsin*** (1773) and bust of Empress Catherine II, one of her best sculptural portrayals (it is a copy of the 1771 original possessed by the Victoria and Albert Museum in London).

Mikhail Kozlovsky (1753–1802) designed the first in Russia monument commemorating not a royal person but celebrated generalissimo Alexander Suvorov (unveiled in the Field of Mars in St Petersburg in 1801). The gallery has a smaller model of the monument.

Fyodor Rokotov (1735?–1808) was noted for his charming portraits. Born in the family of Prince Repnin's serfs, he was enrolled in the St Petersburg Academy of Art and later moved to Moscow where he spent the last forty years of his life. He was commissioned the coronation portrait of Catherine II which she approved and ordered other painters to copy it. His sketch for the portrait is distinguished by a delicate palette. The noble profile of the empress recalls those depicted on antique cameos. His *Unknown Lady in Rose* (early 1770s) reveals inner inspiration and lyricism. The vibrant "smoky" background accentuates the picture's almost monochromatic colour scale. Faces of Rokotov's sitters are often animated with a characteristic mysterious half smile.

Ivan Argunov (1729–1802) came from a family of serf artists and architects. His *Portrait of an Unknown Woman in Russian Peasant Dress* (1784) most probably represents the nurse of the children of Count Sheremetyev, Argunov's landlord. The portrait embodies the Russian ideal of feminine beauty characterized by purity, dignity and calmness.

The oeuvre of **Dmitry Levitsky** (1735–1822), an outstanding portrait painter of the second half of the 18th century, displays an unsurpassed artistic skill and diversity of compositional techniques used to render the psychological characteristics of his models. In the *Portrait of Countess Ursula Mniszek* (1782), its cold colours, stiff pattern of the starched lace and folds of formal dress convey the personality of this beautiful, yet cold and haughty young lady.

The proprietor of metallurgic enterprises in the Urals, Pavel Demidov was a person of facetious wit. As if challenging the public opinion, this eccentric, fabulously rich man poses for his portrait carelessly leaning on a watering can. In the *Portrait of Pavel Demidov* (1773) Levitsky who was a freethinker doesn't hesitate to show his model in a most unusual for Russian formal portraits outfit – a dressing gown and cap. In the age of the Enlightenment portraits were meant to give some moral instruction. The watering can and flowerpots, attributes of a gardener, and the building of the orphanage in the background allegorically illustrate the philanthropic ventures of Demidov who took care not only of flowers but of parentless children (he gave money to the orphanage).

43. Hall of 18th-century sculpture

44. Fedot Shubin (1740–1805)
Portrait of Prince Alexander Golitsin. 1773
Marble. Height 70 cm

45. Dmitry Levitsky (1735–1822)
Portrait of Countess Ursula Mniszek. 1782
Oil on canvas. 72 x 57 cm

46. Dmitry Levitsky (1735–1822)
Portrait of Pavel Demidov. 1773
Oil on canvas. 222 x 166 cm

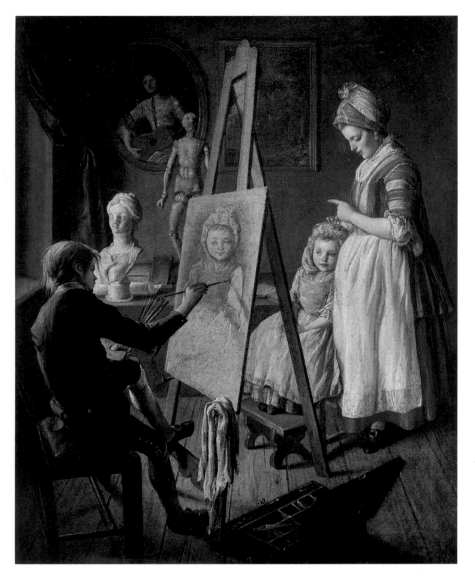

A Young Painter was executed by **Ivan Firsov** (1730 – after 1785) during his visit to Paris (between 1765 and 1768). The painting displays Firsov's shrewd observation and betrays the influence of the renowned French master Jean-Baptiste-Simeon Chardin.

In Russia landscapes were accepted as independent subjects rather late. It was not until 1776 that a landscape class was organized at the Academy of Art. The works of the leading artists of the late 18th – early 19th centuries Semyon Shchedrin (1745–1804), **Fyodor Alexeyev** (1753/1754?–1824) and Fyodor Matveyev (1758–1826) represent different types of landscape painting. Shchedrin mostly produced decorative panels for royal palaces, Alexeyev was celebrated for his panoramic townscapes while Matveyev's Italian views adhere to the Classicist tradition of idealized landscape.

The last great portrait painter of the 18th century was **Vladimir Borovikovsky** (1757–1825). He developed under the influence of a group of Sentimentalist artists and writers and mostly painted small-size intimate portraits. His virtuoso *Portrait of Maria Lopukhina* (1797) illustrates the Sentimentalist ideal of feminine beauty. The young woman seems to indulge in daydreams. The landscape in the background symbolizes the harmony of nature and the pink rose the passing beauty of youth. More imposing and pompous is the formal *Portrait of Prince Alexander Kurakin* (1801–1802), Paul I's vice-chancellor, the famous "diamond" prince.

47. Ivan Firsov (1730 – after 1785)
A Young Painter. Between 1765 and 1768
Oil on canvas. 67 x 55 cm

48. Fyodor Alexeyev (1753/1754 (?)–1824)
The Palace Embankment Viewed from the Sts Peter and Paul Fortress. 1794
Oil on canvas. 70 x 108 cm

49. Vladimir Borovikovsky (1757–1825)
Portrait of Maria Lopukhina. 1797
Oil on canvas. 72 x 53.5 cm

50. Orest Kiprensky (1782–1836)
Portrait of the Poet Alexander Pushkin. 1827
Oil on canvas. 63 x 54 cm

Orest Kiprensky (1782–1836) has most fully expressed in his portraiture the Romantic ideal. His sitters are people of different age and temperament but all of them have a unique inner world and their charm derives from their individuality rather than outward appearance. His early masterworks are the *Portrait of Alexander Chelishchev* (c. 1809) and the *Portrait of Darya Khvostova* (1814). His manner improved after his long sojourn to Italy and visit to Paris. The ***Portrait of Alexander Pushkin*** (1827) demonstrates the artist's impeccable style which has the austerity of Neoclassicism and the sensibility of Romanticism. Faithfully rendering the appearance of the sitter, the artist gives an idealized, generalized image of the poet, "the servant of the Muses," alien to the vanity of the world. The painting was commissioned by Pushkin's close friend Anton Delvig and purchased by the poet as a memento after Delvig's death. Appreciating it as a genuine masterpiece, Pushkin wrote in a poem dedicated to Kiprensky: "I see myself as if in a mirror, but this mirror flattens me."

Silvester Shchedrin (1791–1830) is regarded as a pioneer of plein air landscape in Russian art. He was the first to paint in oils out-of-doors. Upon graduating from the St Petersburg Academy of Art, he moved to Italy and lived there the rest of his life. Shchedrin shows Italy as a sunny fairy-tale land, a picturesque country of eternal summer and happiness. His pictures echoed the Romantic ardour with which Italy was described by Russian poets.

51. Silvester Shchedrin (1791–1830)
New Rome. Castel Sant' Angelo
(Castle of the Holy Angel). 1825
Oil on canvas. 45.6 x 67.2 cm

52. Fyodor Tolstoy (1783–1873)
Red and White Currents. 1818
Gouache on brown paper. 17.4 x 23.8 cm

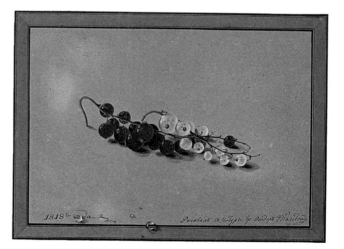

Karl Bryullov (1799–1852) was the most popular artist of his time. He said that a painter must be able to do everything. A virtuoso portraitist, he created imposing historical compositions and monumental wall paintings. He was also an accomplished draughtsman and watercolourist and an innovator who introduced new types of compositions and decorative effects. Bryullov deserved the name of "brilliant Karl" given to him by his contemporaries. His most famous piece, *The Last Day of Pompeii* (1833, possessed by the Russian Museum in St Petersburg), is the manifesto of Romanticism. The gallery has a sketch for the painting. On display are superb portraits by Bryullov. These formal likenesses demonstrate the exalted, rapturous nature of his talent, eager to create majestic, lavish artworks. His ***Rider*** (1832) is a new type of portrait to which the painter has introduced action, eliminating traditional static postures. It portrays Giovannina Paccini (rider) and her cousin Amalia Paccini who were adopted by Countess Julia Samoylova. The portraits of the poet and translator Alexander Strugovshchikov (1840) and the Italian archaeologist Michelangelo Lanci (1851) as well as the ***Self-Portrait*** (1848) executed with rare spontaneity and inspiration are characterized by their psychological profundity and outward splendour.

The oeuvre of **Alexander Ivanov** (1806–1858) was a remarkable phenomenon in Russian art. An original painter and philosopher, he devoted most part of his artistic career to the grandiose composition, ***The Appearance of Christ to the People (The Appearance of the Messiah)*** (1837–1857). The artist produced more than 600 drawings and oil sketches for the composition, some of which were paintings in their own right (***A Branch***, *Olive Trees Near the Cemetery in Albano*. *The New Moon*, *The Bay of Naples* and others). Working out the principles of plein air landscape in these sketches, Ivanov was ahead of contemporary European masters. The subject of the painting is an episode from the Gospels. When St John was baptizing the people, he saw Jesus approaching the Jordan. The painting is not a mere illustration to the New Testament text. Ivanov offers his own interpretation of the event. For him Christ is the Word that has become flesh, the prophecy that has come true and shows the people the path to salvation. He depicts the conflict of attitudes, the conflict of belief and unbelief, the problem of choice between social welfare, evident to everybody, and spiritual freedom, unseen but having the power of transfiguration (personified by the figures of the master and his slave in the centre of the composition). Praising the extraordinary significance of this philosophical work, the art critic Vasily Stasov wrote that Ivanov was one of the greatest personalities that had ever been born.

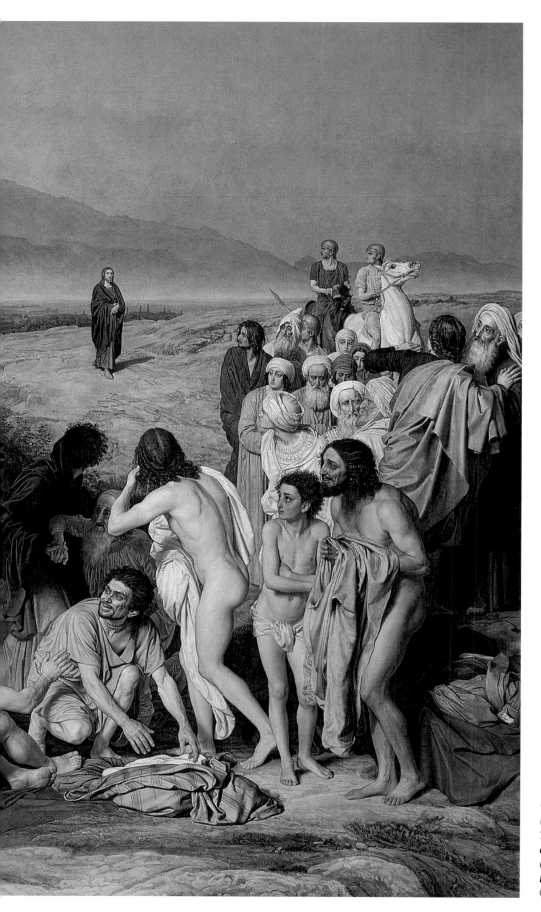

55. Alexander Ivanov
(1806–1858)
**The Appearance
of Christ to the People
(The Appearance of
the Messiah)**. 1837–1857
Oil on canvas. 540 x 750 cm

The artistic pursuits of **Vasily Tropinin** (1776–1857) had a great impact on the formation of the Moscow school of painting. A serf artist, he received freedom at the age of forty-seven and settled in Moscow to become a typical Muscovite in his lifestyle, attitudes and artistic manner. His models are open-hearted and good-natured. They are a bit careless about their dress, their postures are easy. Tropinin succeeded in conveying a special charm and coziness of Moscow life.

His portraits that had much in common with genre painting (*Lace-maker*, 1823 and *Gold Embroiderer*, 1826) enjoyed great popularity. One of the most lyrical works by Tropinin is the *Portrait of the Artist's Son* (*c.* 1818). The warm tones and soft light of his pictures helped him to bring out the individuality of the sitters who were always kind and responsive.

Alexey Venetsianov (1780–1847), another champion of new tendencies in Russian art, was the first to paint scenes from the life of peasantry. He is considered the founder of a new school of training, named after him. His main principle was to render nature as the artist found it. Venetsianov was fascinated by rural life with its seasonal rhythms dictated by the cycles of nature. His everyday scenes are idyllic and meditative. The simplicity and innocence of the subject matter and its idealized, even exalted interpretation, the poetic sense of the divine in nature and man who is seen as essentially part of it echo the attitudes of the early Renaissance artists. The oeuvre of Venetsianov is represented in the gallery by his best paintings, *In the Field*.

56. Alexander Ivanov (1806–1858)
A Branch
Oil on paper pasted on canvas.
46.5 x 62.4 cm

57. Vasily Tropinin (1776–1857)
Lace-maker. 1823
Oil on canvas. 74.7 x 59.3 cm

58. Pyotr Sokolov (1791–1848)
Portrait of Maria Kikina, Princess Volkonskaya in Marriage. 1839
Watercolours, whiting, lead pencil, brush and pen on paper. 55.5 x 41.5 cm

Spring (first half of the 1820s), *Har-vesting. Summer* (mid-1820s) and **Hay-making** (before 1827) donated to the museum in 2002 by the citizen of Great Britain Victor Provatorov.

In his country estate of Safonkovo (Tver province) Venetsianov established an art school for children from poor families where the offspring of serf peasants were admitted. Before that he had invited his poor pupils to live in his St Petersburg apartment. Improving their artistic manner, the talented teacher took special care to maintain and develop their individuality. His most gifted disciples were **Kapiton Zelentsov** (1790–1847), Yevgraf Krendovsky (1810 – after 1853), Fyodor Slavyansky (1819–1876) and Alexey Tyranov (1808–1859). All of them adored their teacher, had a reverential affection for nature and were keen on representing interior and rural scenes.

Pavel Fedotov (1815–1852) was a remarkable genre and portrait painter and draughtsman. He renounced his career of an officer for that of an artist and devoted all his time to painting everyday down-to-earth scenes from the life of the common people. Later he confessed that he had learnt a lot from the satirical and moral engravings of the celebrated English masters William Hogarth and Sir David Wilkie. However, he didn't simply imitate their style but introduced a critical note into Russian painting. In his masterpiece, **The Major's Marriage Proposal** (1848), Fedotov turns out to be a brilliant story-teller and master of explicit detail. He discloses the individuality of his characters by their poses, gestures and motions. When the picture was shown to the public, he even wrote his own comments to it. "The dashing corpulent major, a man without means, hopes to improve his circumstances by marrying a rich merchant's daughter and thinks, while twisting his moustache: 'Soon I'll get the money!'" This scene would appear ungainly but for the unique power of art, able to transform any subject it depicts.

The unfinished composition *Encore, encore!* (1851–1852) was executed shortly before Fedotov's death. It expresses the misery and despondency of the painter who was gravely ill, yet sought new themes for his art.

59. Alexey Venetsianov (1780–1847)
Hay-making. Before 1827
Oil on canvas. 66 x 54 cm

60. Alexey Venetsianov (1780–1847)
In the Field. Spring. First half
of the 1820s
Oil on canvas. 51.2 x 65.5 cm

61. Kapiton Zelentsov (1790–1845)
In the Rooms. Late 1820s
Oil on canvas. 37 x 45.5 cm

62. Pavel Fedotov (1815–1852)
*The Major's Marriage
Proposal*. 1848
Oil on canvas. 58.3 x 75.4 cm

RUSSIAN ART IN THE SECOND HALF OF THE 19TH — EARLY 20TH CENTURIES

The Tretyakov Gallery collection of art from the second half of the 19th century is somewhat a "pictorial encyclopaedia" of Russian life. It is unsurpassed in its artistic quality and variety. All styles and types of national art are fully represented here. Exhibitions on individual artists highlight the work of most illustrious exponents of Russian painting, such as Vasily Perov, Ivan Kramskoy, Ilya Repin, Isaac Levitan, Valentin Serov and others. This section was created in Pavel Tretyakov's lifetime. Its paintings record most important historical events, social changes and outstanding figures of the period who acquired the dominant influence on their contemporaries. Like the literary works of Leo Tolstoy, Fyodor Dostoyevsky and Ivan Turgenev, the paintings collected by Tretyakov make it possible to become acquainted with this period of Russian history and culture.

In the second half of the 19th century art became more and more concerned with social, moral and aesthetic aspects. The works of most of the painters from the period displayed sympathetic attitude towards the hard life of the people. In the mid-19th century there was introduced a new conception of art. According to it, art was not only to reflect reality, but judge and improve it attracting the public attention to its problems and defects. This tendency was first of all manifested in genre painting that showed the tragic life of the lower middle class: petty officials, poor townsfolk, clergy, merchants that began to exert a considerable influence on economy and peasants who were considered free after the abolition of serfdom in 1861.

63. The Vereshchagin Room

64. Vasily Pukirev (1832–1890)
Misalliance. 1862
Oil on canvas. 173 x 136.5 cm

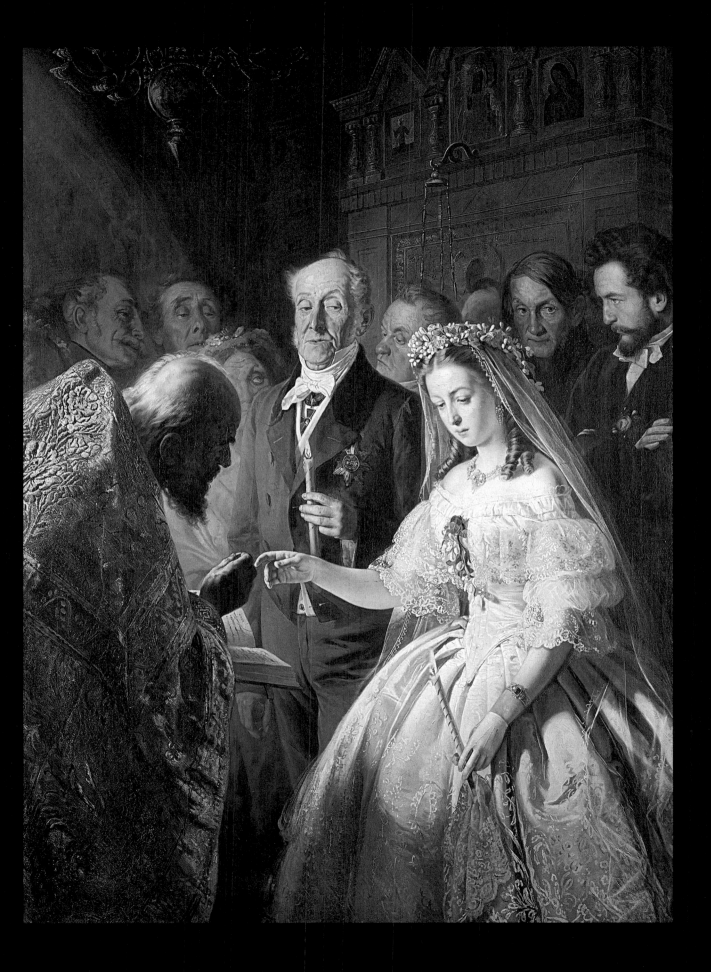

Many painters dealt in their works with the problems widely discussed in Russian literature. ***Jokers. The Merchants'***
Yard in Moscow (1865) by **Illarion Pryanishnikov** (1840–1894) was inspired by Alexander Ostrovsky's play of the
same name. Heated disputes were centered on the ***Misalliance*** (1862) by **Vasily Pukirev** (1832–1890), illustrating the
story of a dowerless girl, the theme of another popular play by Ostrovsky.

Society began to express concern for women's rights. In the 1850s and 1860s women's inequality became a burning
topic of the day which was reflected in the works of many genre painters: *A Sick Musician* (1859) by Mikhail Klodt (1835–
1914), *Interrupted Betrothal* (1860) by Adrian Volkov (1827–1873), *The Ward* (1867) by Nikolay Nevrev (1830–1904),
Before the Wedding by Firs Zhuravlyov (1836–1901) and *The Arrival of a Governess to a Merchant's House* (1866) by Vasily
Perov (1834–1882). At the same time other artists depicted famous women of the past. **Konstantin Flavitsky** (1830–
1866) was interested in the personality of Princess Tarakanova, a Frenchwoman who had claimed she was the daughter of
the unmarried Empress Elizabeth and pretended to the Russian throne. The painter has chosen a romantic, yet unreliable
version of her life-story. According to it, she was imprisoned in the Sts Peter and Paul Fortress and died there during
a flood. Some contemporaries interpreted the painting as an illustration to the popular Romantic theme of fate while
others saw in it the tragic story of a defenceless woman.

In the 1860s – 1870s **Vasily Perov** (1834–1882), the greatest exponent of Russian critical Realism in its initial stage,
was at the height of his career. In his works of the 1860s he ruthlessly, yet with a deep compassion, laid bare the tragedy of
contemporary life, full of sin and social conflicts. His broodings of the wretchedness of the existence, wasted lives and lost
hopes, human suffering in the cruel and unjust world are expressed in his most famous pictures, *The Last Journey (Village*
Funeral) (1865), ***Troyka: Young Apprentices Pulling a Water Barrel*** (1866), *The Last Tavern at the City Gate* (1868) and others.

65. Konstantin Flavitsky (1830–1866)
Princess Tarakanova. 1864
Oil on canvas. 245 x 187.5 cm

66. Illarion Pryanishnikov (1840–1894)
Jokers. The Merchants' Yard in Moscow. 1865
Oil on canvas. 63.4 x 87.5 cm

Perov readily accepted Tretyakov's commission to paint portraits of the playwright Alexander Ostrovsky (1871) and the great novelist **Fyodor Dostoyevsky** (1872). These masterpieces of portraiture are significant for their psychological penetration and expressiveness.

Russian landscape painting fully developed and reached its acme in the second half of the 19th century. Many important discoveries were made and a lot of new techniques introduced when the artists began to work out-of-doors. They came to appreciate their native countryside, the unique beauty of serene Russian nature. Various types of Russian scenery are to be seen in the works of **Alexey Savrasov** (1830–1897), **Fyodor Vasilyev** (1850–1873) and **Ivan Shishkin** (1832–1898). *The Rooks Have Returned* (1871) by Savrasov is a fine specimen of lyrical landscape.

67. Vasily Perov (1834–1882)
Troyka: Young Apprentices Pulling a Water Barrel. 1866
Oil on canvas. 123.5 x 167.5 cm

68. Vasily Perov (1834–1882)
Portrait of the Writer Fyodor Dostoyevsky. 1872
Oil on canvas. 99 x 80.5 cm

69. Alexey Savrasov (1830–1897)
The Rooks Have Returned. 1871
Oil on canvas. 62 x 48.5 cm

70. Ivan Shishkin
(1832–1898)
Rye. 1878
Oil on canvas.
107 x 187 cm

71. Ivan Ayvazovsky
(1817–1900)
***The Black Sea
(The Beginning
of a Storm)***. 1881
Oil on canvas.
149 x 208 cm

The oeuvre of Fyodor Vasilyev, an exceptionally talented artist who died at the age of twenty-three, betrays the influence of French landscapists. Shishkin's landscapes are a paean to Russian nature, its vastness, great expanses and grandeur. "Boundless spaces, vast fields, rye...It is a land of plenty... It is the wealth of Russia," wrote the artist describing his picture ***Rye*** (1878).

"The sea is my life," said **Ivan Ayvazovsky** (1817–1900) who has left thousands of marine paintings. The artist developed his own method of painting. He always worked in the studio, painting from his memory that was phenomenal. He explained that, "the movement of water can't be captured with the brush." Since the 1840s more than 100 exhibitions of his works were held in Europe and America. The Rome, Paris and Amsterdam academies of art were proud to count Ayvazovsky among their members. Tretyakov was not an admirer of his magnificent art but, recognizing his talent and worldwide popularity, he acquired a number of Ayvazovsky's paintings. One of the best is ***The Black Sea (The Beginning of a Storm)*** (1881).

Lev Lagorio (1827–1905) and Alexey Bogolyubov (1824–1896) also have contributed to seascape painting. Bogolyubov travelled a lot round Russia and Europe and lived many years in France. Like Sergey Tretyakov, he was fond of the Barbizon school, collected works of its artists and donated them, together with his own paintings, to the Saratov Art Museum which he had founded.

Ayvazovsky's disciple, a "master of light," **Arkhip Kuinji** (1842–1910) chose almost solely landscapes with luminous effects. Using the laws of optics and his own innovative techniques, he created radiant paintings of moonlit (*Night on the Dnieper*, version of 1882) and sunlit (***The Birch Grove***, 1879) scenes. In most of Kuinji's works their luminescent colours create a special atmosphere of mystery. His style was further developed by one of his renowned students, Nicholas Roerich.

72. Fyodor Vasilyev
(1850–1873)
Wet Meadow. 1872
Oil on canvas.
70 x 114 cm

73. Arkhip Kuinji
(1842–1910)
The Birch Grove. 1879
Oil on canvas.
97 x 181 cm

Dissatisfaction with the academic system gradually grew among young artists. The Academy's role as the guardian of artistic methods and techniques was quite positive but at the same time it cultivated solely Neoclassical art. Works produced within its walls depicted either classical or historical subjects. The young generation of artists who were interested in new ideas and opportunities regarded this policy of the Academy as an encroachment upon their freedom. An organized protest against its stagnant system took place in 1863. It has come down to art history as the "rebellion of the fourteen." A group of fourteen undergraduates left the Academy after they had been rejected the right to choose individual themes (instead of the common classical assignment) for their diploma works. They formed the first independent St Petersburg Association of Artists. All its members were interested in contemporary life and its problems and upheld the principles of progressive art.

In 1870 the Society for Circulating Art Exhibitions (*Peredvizhniki*) was set up by the democratically minded painters of St Petersburg and Moscow. The oeuvre of this most influential group is fully represented in the Tretyakov Gallery.

Ivan Kramskoy (1837–1887) became the ideological leader of the Society. He believed that the true artist was a prophet who was "to hold up to people a mirror, to make their hearts sound the alarm..." His *Christ in the Wilderness* (1872) was shown at the second exhibition of the Society and those who saw it could not but compare the painting with Ivanov's *Appearance of Christ to the People*. According to Kramskoy's idea, Christ who has come down to the people finds himself alone in the wilderness. The picture evoked many religious, philosophical and moral questions. Kramskoy tried to convey the moral tension and suffering of man in his quest for truth, his readiness for self-sacrifice. The painter who looked for an ideal in contemporary life was interested in outstanding personalities of his time, people of dignity, insight, courage, unique inner world. It was by no chance he preferred portraiture to other genres. His well-known lifetime *Portrait of Leo Tolstoy* (1873) shows a man of strong will and powerful intellect. Tolstoy was also impressed by Kramskoy who served as the prototype of the artist Mikhaylov in his novel *Anna Karenina*. Tretyakov and Kramskoy were close friends and the latter

75. Ivan Kramskoy (1837–1887)
Self-portrait. 1867
Oil on canvas. 52.7 x 44 cm

76. Ivan Kramskoy (1837–1887)
Unknown Lady. 1883. Oil on canvas. 75.5 x 99 cm

74. Vasily Maximov (1844–1911)
A Magician Coming to a Peasants' Wedding. 1875
Oil on canvas. 116 x 188 cm. Detail

80. Vasily Surikov (1848–1916)
Boyarynya Morozova. 1887
Oil on canvas. 304 x 587.5 cm

81. Ilya Repin (1844–1930)
Portrait of the Composer Modest Mussorgsky. 1881
Oil on canvas. 69 x 57 cm

82. Ilya Repin (1844–1930)
Religious Procession in the Province of Kursk. 1881–1883
Oil on canvas. 175 x 280 cm

83. Ilya Repin (1844–1930)
Ivan the Terrible and His Son Ivan. 16 November, 1581. 1885
Oil on canvas. 199.5 x 254 cm

84. Mark Antokolsky (1843–1902)
Tsar Ivan the Terrible. 1875
Marble. Height 151 cm

This woman of noble birth fiercely opposed the reforms of Patriarch Nikon which led to the church schism in the mid-17th century.

Surikov portrays the moment when Morozova in chains is carried down Moscow streets to be sent to a convent. This epic work is characterized by profound psychological revelation and exquisite colours.

Ilya Repin (1844–1930) was the greatest Realist painter. The Tretyakov Gallery possesses more than 150 paintings and a collection of drawings, watercolours and pastels by Repin who has left a large and varied artistic heritage. His monumental impressive *Religious Proces-*

sion in the Province of Kursk (1881–1883) was the result of the artist's observations of Russia's contemporary life with its sharp social conflicts. It shows a large crowd of people following the miracle-working icon which contains a variety of social types.

Ivan the Terrible and His Son Ivan. 16 November, 1581 (1885) was painted after the assassination of Emperor Alexander I by revolutionary terrorists from "People's Will" group in spring, 1881. The date (1581) in the picture's title evoked associations with the tragic event of 1881 and the bloody campaign of repression that followed it. *They Didn't Expect Him* (1884–1888) shows a political exile coming home after a long separation from his family. Repin has chosen the culmination of the story, the sudden return and the psychological reaction of every character. Portraits of Russian intellectuals constitute a remarkable part of Repin's oeuvre. **Portrait of the Composer Modest Mussorgsky** (1881) is a genuine masterpiece. Repin's significance in Russian art is comparable to that of Tolstoy in Russian literature. The latter was his intimate friend, and Repin painted a number of his portraits showing the great writer at work and rest.

The best specimen of sculpture from the period is **Tsar Ivan the Terrible** (1875) by **Mark Antokolsky** (1843–1902). The public was fascinated by the statue. Ivan Turgenev wrote: "The impression is so profound... One can no longer imagine Ivan the Terrible in any mien but that created by Antokolsky's fancy."

The art of **Nikolay Gay** (1831–1894) dealt with the moral problems of his day. In his ***Peter I Interrogating Tsarevich Alexey Petrovich in Peterhof*** (1871) he shows that the progress of history is determined by the struggle between opposing ideas and attitudes. This theme acquired great importance for Gay. He was seriously influenced by the didactic teachings of Tolstoy with whom he was on close terms. His later, rather innovative, works (***"What is Truth?"***, 1890, and ***The Calvary***, 1893) are tragic and gloomy. He uses the figure of Christ to express his own philosophical idea that it is impossible to help people and make them better, without suffering.

85. Nikolay Gay (1831–1894)
"What is Truth?" Christ and Pilate. 1890
Oil on canvas. 233 x 171 cm

86. Nikolay Gay (1831–1894)
Peter I Interrogating Tsarevich Alexey Petrovich in Peterhof. 1871
Oil on canvas. 135.7 x 173 cm

87. Nikolay Gay (1831–1894)
The Calvary. 1893
Oil on canvas. 222.4 x 191.8 cm

Like other members of the Abramtsevo group formed round the famous philanthropist Savva Mamontov, **Vasily Polenov** (1844–1927) had a variety of talents. He was a painter, architect, stage-set designer and decorator. According to his own words, landscape painting with elements of genre scenes was his favourite art form. Polenov's fondness for tranquil scenery was close to that of the well-known novelist Turgenev who highly valued his works. The artist loved Moscow and its vicinity. His landscapes (***A Courtyard in Moscow***, *Granny's Garden*, both 1878, and *Overgrown Pond*, 1879) are fresh, airy and gleam with light. The *Life of Christ* series (late 1890s – early 1900s) presents the artist's ideal of eternal spiritual beauty.

The oeuvre of **Isaac Levitan** (1860–1900) is justifiably compared to the literary works of Anton Chekhov, his close friend. Most of his landscapes contain no figures, but the realm of nature is inseparable for him from the realm of human feelings. He was a recognized master of emotional landscape, as he rendered states of nature, consonant with the subtlest human emotions. His Volga journey imparted epic grandeur and philosophical depth to his paintings (*Plios. After the Rain*, 1889, ***Evening Bells***, 1892, and *Eternal Rest*, 1894). The famous ***Golden Autumn*** (1895) and *Spring Flood* (1897) are sincere and optimistic. In the last years of his life when the artist was gravely ill, his landscapes became more laconic and refined and mostly portrayed twilit or moonlit scenes.

88. Vasily Polenov (1844–1927)
A Courtyard in Moscow. 1878
Oil on canvas. 64.5 x 80.1 cm

89. Isaac Levitan (1860–1900)
Evening Bells. 1892
Oil on canvas. 87 x 107.6 cm

90. Isaac Levitan (1860–1900)
Golden Autumn. 1895
Oil on canvas. 82 x 126 cm

The turn of the century was a time of vigorous innovative developments in Russian art which had a point of contact with European artistic process. There arose dozens of new styles, trends and groups. The oeuvre of **Mikhail Vrubel** (1856–1910), one of most original avant-garde artists, was the first and most brilliant manifestation of Symbolism in Russian visual culture. He was involved in the artistic pursuits of the Abramtsevo group which had a nationalistic tendency. The artist widely used motifs from the Russian national epic and folk culture when he created decorative panels and majolica sculpture, designed stage-sets and costumes for the Russian Private Opera and painted balalaikas. The subject of the demon had a special fascination for Vrubel (**The Demon Seated**, 1890, *The Defeated Demon*, 1902, and others). These paintings did not simply embody the artist's individualistic attitude and his search for "new" spirituality or were inspired by Lermontov's famous poem and Rubinstein's opera. The theme was most characteristic of the art of Symbolism.

Vrubel worked much in monumental painting technique. He produced series of decorative panels for some Moscow mansions. For the All-Russia Exposition of Industrial and Artistic Design held in Nizhny Novgorod in 1896 he painted two huge panels, one based on *La Princesse Lointaine* by Edmond Rostand and the other *Mikula Selyaninovich* interpreting themes of Russian folk tales. Both of them were rejected by the academic jury of the exposition, yet purchased by the art patron Savva Mamontov. Later *La Princesse Lointaine* found its way to the Tretyakov Gallery where it was hung in a spacious hall specially designed for it, while still nothing is known about the second panel.

Vrubel was a talented portraitist, accomplished draughtsman and watercolourist. He had a highly individual artistic manner. His colour scheme was dominated by gleaming lilac and violet colours which were most appropriate for the portrayal of night scenes (*Pan*, 1898, *Nightfall*, 1900, *Lilac*, 1901, and **The Swan-Princess**, 1900). Besides the magic charm of colours, his style is distinguished by a unique brushwork imitating mosaics.

91. The Mikhail Vrubel Room which contains the panel **La Princesse Lointaine**. 1896
Oil on canvas. 750 x 1400 cm

92. Mikhail Vrubel (1856–1910)
The Swan-Princess. 1900. Oil on canvas. 142.5 x 93.5 cm

93. Mikhail Vrubel. (1856–1910)
The Demon Seated. 1890
Oil on canvas. 114 x 211 cm

94. Nicholas Roerich (1874–1947)
Messenger. Kin has Risen Against Kin. 1897
Oil on canvas. 124.7 x 184.3 cm

95. Andrey Ryabushkin (1861–1904)
17th-century Russian Women in a Church. 1899
Oil on canvas. 53.5 x 68.8 cm

96. Mikhail Nesterov (1862–1942)
The Vision of Young Bartholomew. 1889–1890
Oil on canvas. 160 x 211 cm

Nicholas Roerich (1874–1947) fashioned his reputation as an artist, philosopher, writer, traveller and public figure. He lived an eventful life devoted to spiritual quests. Born in Russia, he toured Europe and America and later wandered through Asia. He meditated much on the links connecting past and present, man and the universe and his ideas were formed into a teaching that had many supporters and followers. He became some sort of a guru and preacher. He painted historical (**Battle**, 1906) and architectural landscapes, created a series of pictures on the theme of pagan cultures of the Slavs and their neighbours (*Red Sailes. Prince Vladimir's Campaign at Korsun,* 1900; *The Beginning of Rus. The Slavs, Guests from Overseas,* 1901, *The Town is being Built,* 1902; *The Slavs on the Dnieper,* 1905, and *The Death of a Viking,* 1908). The first painting in the series (***Messenger. Kin has Risen Against Kin***, 1897) illustrates one of the episodos from the famous Russian 12th-century chronicle *Tale of Bygone Years.*

Historicism, a major and most influential trend in contemporary art, inspired Roerich with a fondness for early Russian painting and the past of the country. The artist employed old Russian motifs in the decoration of the Talashkino estate in the vicinity of Smolensk and stage-set designs for Diaghilev's Ballets Russes in Paris. In his later years he took interest in Oriental cultures and religions, particularly Buddhism. In 1925–1928 he organized the famous Central Asian Expedition and founded the Institute of Himalayan Studies in India where he permanently lived from 1930 till his death. His works from the period, meditative and symbolical, illustrate his religious views.

The oeuvre of **Mikhail Nesterov** (1862–1942) was in the mainstream of Christian tradition, he believed that Russian national ideology was based on Orthodox Christianity. He painted a lot of murals and icons for churches. Among his best works is a series of paintings devoted to St Sergius of Radonezh (*Hermit,* 1888–1898; ***The Vision of Young Bartholomew***, 1889–1890 and *The Young Years of St Sergius,* 1892–1897). His canvas *In Russia (The Soul of the People)*(1914–1916) gives a generalized and idealized image of Russia as God-seeker. The depicted characters include a tsar wearing the Monomachus cap, a metropolitan (archpriest), a monk, a fool for Christ's sake, an invalid soldier and nurses as well as the writers Fyodor Dostoyevsky and Leo Tolstoy and the religious philosopher Vladimir Solovyov (the last on the right). He was remarkable portraitist who strove to reveal the spirit and loftiness of his models. In the 1910s – 1930s he painted a number of portraits of Russian intellectuals, the people who devoted all their life to creative work.

97. Andrey Ryabushkin (1861–1904)
***Wedding Procession in Moscow
(17th Century)***. 1901
Oil on canvas. 90 x 206.5 cm

98. Philip Malyavin (1869–1940)
The Whirlwind. 1906
Oil on canvas. 223 x 410 cm

99. Igor Grabar (1871–1960)
March Snow. 1904
Oil on canvas. 80 x 62 cm

In 1903 the Union of Russian Artists was established by Abram Arkhipov (1862–1930), Apollinary Vasnetsov (1856–1933), Sergey Vinogradov (1869–1938) and Sergey Ivanov (1864–1910). Later it was joined by **Igor Grabar** (1871–1960), Stanislav Zhukovsky (1873–1944), **Philip Malyavin** (1869–1940), Arkady Rylov (1870–1939), Konstantin Yuon (1875–1958) and many others. They developed the principles of realistic plein air painting. Their prevalent art form was landscape with genre elements (elements from everyday life), or lyrical landscape in Levitan's tradition and they also produced works in the style of Russian Impressionism. The manner of the Moscow members of the Union was characterized by thick brushstrokes, subtle tones and the suffusion of the scenery with light. After 1910 they constituted the larger part of the Union which contributed much to the development of Russian painting, particularly its Moscow school.

100. Valentin Serov (1865–1911)
Portrait of Henrietta Girshman. 1907
Tempera on canvas. 140 x 140 cm

101. Valentin Serov (1865–1911)
Girl with Peaches (*Portrait of Vera Mamontova*). 1887
Oil on canvas. 91 x 85 cm

102. Valentin Serov (1865–1911)
The Rape of Europa. 1910
Oil on canvas. 71 x 98 cm

Valentin Serov (1865–1911) was a prolific, hard-working artist and a pace-setter in Russian art whose work had a great impact on contemporary painters. His versatile talent is manifest in his works distinguished by a refined, yet restrained palette and precise draughtsmanship. Contemporaries admired his honesty in art. His early ***Girl with Peaches*** (1887) and *Girl in the Sunlight* (1888) are samples of what can be called Serov's Impressionism.

In the 1890s – 1900s he did portraits of actors, writers and artists. He also received commissions from the royal family, aristocracy and bourgeoisie. In his portraits of high society the artist is a bit ironic about their pretensions and love of luxury. All the portraits are marked by deliberate outspokenness of characterization and reveal the essence of their personalities (*Portrait of Grand Duke Pavel Alexandrovich*, 1897, **Portrait of Henrietta Girshman**, 1907, and *Portrait of Vladimir Girshman*, 1911). Serov evolved his own style of formal portraiture, its imposing forms being in keeping with the great personalities it depicted (portraits of the renowned actress Maria Yermolova and the famous opera singer Fyodor Chaliapin, both 1905). His more intimate portraits of the artist Korovin (1891) and the Morozov family are expressive and have a vigorous saturated colour scale.

Serov employs a vast range of styles, from Impressionism and the decorativeness of Matisse's Post-Impressionism (*Portrait of Ivan Morozov*, 1910) to the linear ornamental patterns of Art Nouveau with elements of classical Greek art (**The Rape of Europa**, *Odysseus and Nausicaä*, both 1910).

Not only painters were inspired by the art of ancient Greece. A number of works by the sculptor Sergey Konenkov (1874–1971) have a somewhat antique flavour (*The Winged Figure* and *Female Torso*, both 1913).

103. Konstantin Korovin (1861–1939)
Paris. Boulevard de Capucines. 1911
Oil on canvas. 73.3 x 60.2 cm

104. Konstantin Korovin (1861–1939)
Fish, Wine and Fruit. 1916
Oil on canvas. 64.7 x 86.8 cm

105. Pavel (Paolo) Trubetskoy (1866–1938)
A Lady Seated
(Jadwiga Von Viller). 1898
Bronze. Height 39 cm

   In Russia, like in Europe, Impressionism "hypnotized a whole generation." Its most illustrious exponents in Russian art were the members of the Union of Russian Artists, particularly the painter **Konstantin Korovin** (1861–1939) and the sculptor **Pavel (Paolo) Trubetskoy** (1866–1938).
   Korovin was the first of Russian artists to turn to Impressionism (*Portrait of a Choir Girl*, 1883) and soon became its ardent supporter. He was keen on rendering the effects of the atmosphere coloured by the reflections of light and devised compositions to capture the light and atmosphere of the fleeting moment, to show the vibration of air. His vigour is manifest even in his still lifes. He loved Paris, its art and the picturesque life of its boulevards and restaurants and painted this city often and with great enthusiasm (*Paris, Paris. Cafe de la Paix*, both 1906 *Paris at Night. Boulevard des Italiens*, 1908, ***Paris. Boulevard de Capucines***, 1911, and others). Korovin was also a stage-set designer, monumental artist and architect. In 1923 he settled in France and lived and worked there as a scenery designer until his death.
   An important event in the artistic life of the turn of the century was the organization of the World of Art group by St Petersburg's educated elité (1898–1904; 1910–1924). Its ideological leaders were Sergey Diaghilev and Alexander Benois who issued the magazine of the same name.

Members of the group criticized the art of the *Peredvizhniki* who, as they thought, "attached too much importance to social problems." They upheld the idea of "art for art's sake" and proclaimed "fancy... culture and taste" their main values. They displayed a special interest in the past and intended to revive the "golden age" of Russian culture. In the early 20th century they were often described as "retrospective dreamers." Almost all eminent artists of the period took part in the World of Art exhibitions, its core members were **Alexander Benois** (1870–1960), **Konstantin Somov** (1869–1939), **Lev (Leon) Bakst (Rosenberg)** (1866–1924) and Mstislav Dobuzhinsky (1875–1957). In the 1910s it was joined by **Boris Kustodiyev** (1878–1927) and **Zinaida Serebryakova** (1884–1967).

106. Evgeny Lanceray (1875–1946)
Empress Elizabeth Petrovna in Tsarskoye Selo. Sketch for an illustration to Alexander Benois' book "The History of Tsarskoye Selo." 1905
Gouache on paper pasted on cardboard. 43 x 61 cm

107. Leon Bakst (1866–1924)
Salomé. Sketch for the costume of Salomé in Oscar Wilde's play of the same name. 1908
Lead pencil and gouache on paper. 46.5 x 29.9 cm

108. Alexander Benois (1870–1960)
The King Takes a Stroll. 1906
Gouache and lead pencil on paper pasted on cardboard. 48 x 62 cm

109. Boris Kustodiyev (1878–1927)
Fair. 1906
Gouache on paper pasted on cardboard. 66.5 x 88.5 cm

110. Alexander Golovin (1863–1930)
***Portrait of the Singer Fyodor Chaliapin
as Holofernes in Alexander Serov's Opera
"Judith."*** 1908
Tempera and pastel on canvas. 163.5 x 212 cm

111. Zinaida Serebryakova (1884–1967)
At Breakfast. 1914
Oil on canvas. 88.5 x 107 cm

112. Konstantin Somov (1869–1939)
***Portrait of a Lady in Blue (Portrait
of the Artist Elizabeth Martynova).***
1897–1900
Oil on canvas. 103 x 103 cm

113. Victor Borisov-Musatov (1870–1905)
The Reservoir. 1902
Tempera on canvas. 177 x 216 cm

Theatre and music had a great impact on the visual arts of the period. **Alexander Golovin** (1863–1930), an outstanding stage-set designer, applied the principles of scenery design to easel painting. One of Golovin's best theatrical portraits which demonstrates his talent of decorator as well is the ***Portrait of Chaliapin as Holofernes in Serov's Opera "Judith"*** (1908). The artist's imaginary landscapes have nothing to do with real nature but look like fanciful dreams. Bakst, Dobuzhinsky and Benois were also talented stage-set designers.

Victor Borisov-Musatov (1870–1905) explored the implications of musical analogies for painting, which was most characteristic of Symbolism that considered music "the foundation of life and art." His canvases (*The Tapestry*, 1901, **The Reservoir**, 1902, *Ghosts*, 1903, and *The Emerald Necklace*, 1903–1904) seem to incorporate music and show the dream-like world of musical elegies. Their harmony is created by subtle colours, with predominating blue that represents the realm of spirit in the art of Symbolists, the rhythm of flowing lines and well-organized compositions.

114. Nikolay Sapunov (1880–1912)
Still Life: Vases, Flowers and Fruit. 1912
Tempera on canvas. 147.2 x 115.8 cm

115. Pavel Kuznetsov (1878–1968)
Evening in the Steppe. 1912
Oil on canvas. 95 x 103 cm

116. Alexander Matveyev (1878–1960)
Calm. 1905
Coloured alabaster. 31.7 x 34.2 x 28.6 cm

The last rooms in the Tretyakov Gallery building in Lavrushinsky Lane house the works by the "Blue Rose" main members: **Pavel Kuznetsov** (1878–1968), **Martiros Saryan** (1880–1972), Nikolay Krymov (1884–1958), Pyotr Utkin (1877–1934), **Nikolay Sapunov** (1880–1912), Sergey Sudeykin (1882–1946) and the sculptor **Alexander Matveyev** (1878–1960).

The group owes its name to the name of its first exhibition held in Moscow in 1907. Originally, it might have been inspired by the symbol of the blue flower in Novalis' Romantic works, or might have been suggested by the Symbolist poet Valery Bryusov, or even might evoke associations with Konstantin Balmont's poem of the same name. However, its literary source has nothing to do with the art production of the group, except that blue colour is widely used in it.

All painters of the "Blue Rose" paid homage to theatre and Sudeykin and Sapunov even made scenery design their profession. The works of the group reveal the influence of French Post-Impressionism and Fauvism, particularly Gauguin and Matisse who prompted Kuznetsov and Saryan to use oriental motifs (Kuznetsov's ***Evening in the Steppe***, 1912, from his Kirghiz series as well as *Street in Constantinople at Noon*, 1910, and *A Date-Palm*, 1911, painted by Saryan after his journey to Turkey and Egypt). Some tendencies (expressive decor, motifs of primitive art) introduced by the "Blue Rose" painters were further developed in pre-revolutionary art.

117. Martiros Saryan (1880–1972)
A Date-Palm. Egypt. 1911
Tempera on cardboard. 106 x 71 cm

RUSSIAN ART IN THE 20TH CENTURY

Russian art in the 20th century embraces a wide variety of styles, attitudes, movements and trends. The new exhibition of the Tretyakov Gallery on Krymsky Val forms a full survey of 20th-century art without dividing it into pre-revolutionary (before 1917) and post-revolutionary (after 1917) periods. It covers almost a century, from 1910 to the early 1990s, and traces the evolution of national art in all its aspects. Even art connoisseurs will learn a lot from this new exposition of contemporary art.

The Russian avant-garde of the 1910s – 1920s has become part of modern artistic culture. Nowadays, works by its artists, recognized abroad long time ago, are well-represented in the Tretyakov Gallery.

The exhibition which features paintings of major trends of the period demonstrates the conflicting character of the 1920s when numerous groups of different stylistic and aesthetic principles claimed their right to be more properly of their time than others. The contest went on in the 1930s though it ceased to be official or legal as many artists were persecuted by the Communists. In the Tretyakov Gallery paintings by representatives of Social Realism are arrayed along with works of the artists who were out of the mainstream of official art.

The art of the second half of the 20th century is no less versatile. The paintings exhibited in these rooms are the works of our contemporaries. Though the 1970s and 1980s are still fresh in our mind, it is for the first time that paintings of different trends from the period are shown together.

So-called metaphoric, or associative, art, praised by the official Moscow Union of Artists as an innovation, is represented next to Conceptual art which had remained in the underground until the 1980s. The exhibition contains traditionally realistic paintings as well.

The Tretyakov Gallery presents not only well-known artists but those who languished in oblivion in the Soviet era. It makes it possible to see the evolution of Russian art without any gaps and highlights its achievements as well as losses.

The exhibition discloses the origins of the Russian avant-garde, illustrating the quest for new forms that led to an unprecedented flowering of nonrepresentational art.

Kuzma Petrov-Vodkin (1878–1939) strove to combine traditional and experimental elements in his oeuvre. A disciple of Valentin Serov, he was influenced by German Symbolism. His artistic career started in the 1900s and in his early years he attempted at subordinating his innovative forms to the ideological essence of painting, which was characteristic of traditional art. ***Bathing the Red Horse*** (1912) represents the artist at his mature best. The picture seems to challenge Impressionism which was extremely popular among the artist's contemporaries. There is nothing casual in it, its colours and images draw on the tradition of early Russian art. The picture reveals the search for spirituality and eternal values.

118. Kuzma Petrov-Vodkin (1878–1939)
Bathing the Red Horse. 1912
Oil on canvas. 160 x 186 cm

119. Robert Falk (1886–1958)
Red Furniture. 1920. Oil on canvas. 105 x 123 cm

120. Natalya Goncharova (1881–1962)
Winter. Picking up Brushwood. 1911. Oil on canvas. 132 x 103 cm

121. Mikhail Larionov (1881–1964)
Soldier at Rest. 1911. Oil on canvas. 119 x 122 cm

The oeuvre of Petrov-Vodkin reflected the process of synthesis or unification of different arts and artistic movements which took place in the 1900s – 1910s. In the early 20th century the poet Vyacheslav Ivanov wrote: "a painting wants to be a fresco."

Natalya Goncharova (1881–1962) and **Mikhail Larionov** (1881–1964) also aspired to achieve a synthesis of art forms. Unlike Petrov-Vodkin, they employed the principles of folk culture, street theatre, sumptuous pageant. In Goncharova's painting the theme of Russia finds its expression in the scenes of rural life where a Russian village personifies all Russia. She frequently depicts seasonal occupations, typical of peasants' life, but makes them more significant and elevated. The contrast of the figures and pictorial space organizes the composition (**Winter. Picking up Brushwood**, 1911). Goncharova achieved the desired synthesis by creating new forms of current styles: Primitivism, German Expressionism and French Post-Impressionism. Primitive art with its archaic nature and wildness had a special appeal to her. Her interest in Primitivism shared by many Russian and Western artists resided in a tendency to repudiate the established academic tradition and its painting techniques. These artists appreciated folk art which was innocent, sincere, free to choose among various artistic methods and simple, devoid of meditations. Goncharova, as if longing to become one of her folk characters herself, thoroughly studied primitive art and tried to understand it, which made her works more serious, even dramatic.

Many artists who drew on primitive art did not stylize their oeuvre but interpreted the style, making it the subject of their painting. Larionov wrote that an artist could portray not only realty but the art of other painters as well. As a disciple of Isaac Levitan and Valentin Serov, he was attracted by the folk core of primitive art, he was particularly fond of shop signboards, popular prints and street theatre. Larionov is ironic and mocking, yet good-natured in his pictures. He often makes use of the grotesque. In his **Soldier at Rest** (1911) he accentuates the passionate, ferocious nature of his hero.

The "Jack of Diamonds" exhibition was held in 1910. The leading artists of the Russian avant-garde (Chagall, Malevich, Popova and others) and famous European painters (Picasso, Braque, Delaunay, Léger and Derain) took part in the show whose original name was suggested by Larionov. The exhibition was organized as a protest against the excessive refinement of the "Blue Rose" and the stylishness of magazine illustrations. Besides, Larionov had a fancy for playing cards which he considered a type of popular prints. The name of the exhibition was to demonstrate that a number of young artists drew strength from primitive, or low, art. The extravagant manner of Larionov and his circle and their use of simplified forms were to reject academic art and its exponents. Members of the group believed that art should serve no didactic purpose as it had been doing since the 19th century. They resolved pictorial tasks without attempting to create pictures of significant social content. They violated the accepted norms as they needed the maximum amount of freedom to create "new art."

Soon Larionov and Goncharova broke away from "Jack of Diamonds." At a discussion in 1912 Larionov called its core members, Konchalovsky, Falk, Kuprin, Lentulov and Mashkov, academicians and reactionaries who blindly followed Cézanne.

The classicized oeuvre of **Robert Falk** (1886–1958) represented what irritated Larionov so much. For him art was a matter of expression. The real event it portrayed did not matter at all. He focused on the emotional and colour aspects of painting. All his works have psychological complexity. Even when he depicts interiors (**Red Furniture**, 1920), it seems that every object has a character of its own. Falk considered this picture his best. He worked on it when suffering from depression after some tragic circumstances in his life. He used a disturbing red colour, dynamic brushwork and numerous associations to convey his anguish and reflections on the difficult and contradictory time he lived in.

The prevalent genre for the artists of "Jack of Diamonds" was still life, for example *Pink Flowers against the Black Background*, 1918, by Alexander Kuprin (1880–1960) and *Still Life with a Bottle of Liqueur*, 1913, by Vasily Rozhdestvensky (1884–1963). It was in this art form that the painters of the group searched for a new expressive idiom, analyzed the system of Cézanne and assimilated the latest methods of French painting, primarily Cubism.

The style of "Jack of Diamonds" was formed under the influence of folk art as well as modern French painting. Thus **Ilya Mashkov** (1881–1944) was infatuated by Cézanne and Matisse. He had a love of bold colours and made them twice as intense as normal (which was typical of Fauvism). As if playing with visual forms, he portrayed real objects as some sort of dummies. In his self-portrait Mashkov looks not like a member of elité but rather like a ship-owner and seems to be proud of this (**Self-Portrait**, 1911). The oeuvre of Mashkov is marked with optimism and cheerfulness, characteristic of all painters from "Jack of Diamonds," which distinguishes them from the reflexivity and preciosity of the "World of Art."

Another founder-member of "Jack of Diamonds" was **Pyotr Konchalovsky** (1876–1956). He lived abroad for long periods, mingled with the artistic elité, invited French painters to take part in exhibitions of his group and was on close terms with Wassily Kandinsky. In his ***Self-Portrait with the Artist's Family (Sienese Self-Portrait)*** (1912) Konchalovsky, like Mashkov, represents himself not as a bohemian but as a private person amid his near and dear during their visit to Italy. The style of the picture is evocative of early Renaissance Italian frescoes. It also reveals the influence of folk art and the Fauvist expressiveness of colour. Konchalovsky employs the method of portraying figures on one canvas from different viewpoints, known in ancient art. The picture combines elements of different styles and schools, which was characteristic of the 1910s when Russian artists in a short period adopted everything achieved by European visual culture since the 1870s.

Of all the members of "Jack of Diamonds," **Aristarkh Lentulov** (1882–1943) was closer than others to the principles of new art. His oeuvre marked the borderline between figurative and non-representational art. In his Paris period he was fond of Cubism. Making use of its distorted shapes, he, however, did not adopt the Cubist interest in the structure of form, which earned him the sobriquet "Futurist a la russe."

In the 1910s Lentulov painted a number of townscapes, all of which included old Russian churches (***Cathedral of St Basil***

THE TRETYAKOV GALLERY

122. Pyotr Konchalovsky
(1876–1956)
**Self-Portrait with
the Artist's Family
(Sienese Self-Portrait)**. 1912
Oil on canvas. 215 x 289 cm

123. Ilya Mashkov (1881–1944)
Self-Portrait. 1911
Oil on canvas. 137 x 107 cm

124. Aristarkh Lentulov
(1882–1943)
**Cathedral of St Basil
the Blessed**. 1913
Oil on canvas, paper cutouts.
170.5 x 163.5 cm

the Blessed, 1913) that were portrayed as some fantastic structures, immaterial and weight-less. His shifted planes and architectural volumes with their linear and colour contrasts and objects shown from different viewpoints were woven into rhythmical patterns conveying the dynamism and bustle of urban life. As if in a kaleidoscope created by someone's fancy his fairy-tale towns unfolded before the viewer. The artist called this method "colour dynamics." He was aware of the similarity between music and colour and took interest in the work of Skriabin who had produced examples of colour music.

The activities of "Jack of Diamonds" and the oeuvre of Goncharova and Larionov initiated the formation of an absolutely new visual language. While in the second half of the 19th century the creed of Russian art was social consciousness, at the turn of the century an aesthetic approach to art and the theory of art as form were dominant. The *Peredvizhniki* insisted on the realistic portrayal of life, believed art to be a vehicle for expressing social ideals, their paintings represented narrative themes.

In the early 20th century art ceased to be the representation of life, artists were interested in it as form, it was art for art's sake. In Symbolism art was not adopted to telling a story, the narrative was obscure and gave rise to a variety of interpretations. For Larionov, Goncharova and other members of "Jack of Diamonds," the subject of their painting was of little importance. What did matter was form. Compositions were based not on the narrative but colours, lines, space... The more independence they got, the more attractive for the artists they became.

This process is reflected in the oeuvre of **Marc Chagall** (1887–1985). Colour is no longer used to characterize the portrayed reality. It, like the composition, is a visual metaphor. Chagall's figurative elements are distributed on the canvas in an arbitrary fashion and it seems that the top and the bottom have been interchanged. Not constrained by gravity, people are flying above a provincial town which lives its own life, but very few of them succeed in rising up to the clouds as the painter and his wife have done (*Above the Town*, 1914–1918).

The 1910s – 1920s was the analytical period in Russian art. All major artists tried to create their own theories of art and sought for a new expressive idiom, both in theory and practice. It was then that the Russian avant-garde was formed. Its painters did not concentrate on human feelings and relations but sought for some other, "higher," values. Art was not to portray reality, but organize it. The artists did not want to tell stories about life. New scientific and technological discoveries had a profound impact on the artists' worldview which ceased to be positivist. The existing reality was interpreted in absolutely new terms (**Alexandra Exter** (1882–1949). *Venice*, 1918).

Pavel Filonov (1883–1941) has created his own ideology of analytical art, opposed to other modern theories. According to him, the process of study is an integral part of the creative process. Only studying the laws of nature, the artist can see the structure of form. Instead of the term "creativity" he introduces the term "sdelannost'" (the quality of being well-made, "madeness"). Art is to imitate the process of life which consists of natural metamorphoses, so the painting must develop like any living organism does. The artist should work on his intellect to comprehend the inner psychic process, the laws of the birth and the death of various forms of life, he must have his own philosophical theory. Filonov distinguishes "the eye that sees" from "the eye that knows." The former is responsible for rendering form and colour, the latter for an intuitive understanding of the inner processes of life. An example of this method is the canvas *Ships* (1913–1915) included by the artist into the 1919 series *Entrance into the World's Flowering*.

125. Marc Chagall (1887–1985)
Above the Town. 1914–1918
Oil on canvas. 141 x 188 cm

126. Alexandra Exter
(1882–1949)
Venice. 1918
Oil on canvas. 268 x 639 cm
Detail

127. Pavel Filonov (1883–1941)
Composition. Ships.
1913–1915
Oil on canvas. 117 x 154 cm

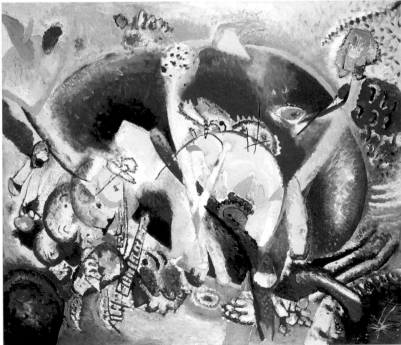

128. Wassily Kandinsky (1866–1944)
The Dim. 1917
Oil on canvas. 105 x 134 cm

129. Wassily Kandinsky (1866–1944)
Improvisation of Cold Forms. 1914
Oil on canvas. 119 x 139 cm

130. Kazimir Malevich (1878–1935)
Portrait of Mikhail Matyushin. 1913
Oil on canvas. 106.5 x 106.5 cm

The next stage in art evolution was nonrepresentational, nonobjective art in which the portrayal of things from the visible world played no part. Abstract art had its origins in Russia. The first purely abstract picture containing no recognizable objects was painted by **Wassily Kandinsky** (1866–1944) in 1910. He is considered the founder of abstract art. His style anticipated Abstract Expressionism. The artist believed that a new era of spirituality was to come soon and people must get prepared for it. According to Kandinsky, contemporary art was to make their conscience free and draw their attention from the realm of nature and the physical world existence. Instead of representing the appearances of objects, the artist should evoke deep emotions by strong colours. Kandinsky thought that the artist must thoroughly study nature but must not simply copy its forms and represent them on canvas (***Improvisation of Cold Forms***, 1914). For Kandinsky every painting was a whole world emerging from chaos and an artist was a creator who should always keep in mind his mission. His compositions done in a slashing, splashing style were balanced and well-organized. Their pulsating, flowing or immobile colours and lines sometimes recalled the objects of the real world but this was of little significance for the artist. He spoke with man and about man but did not tell stories about life. His art is expressive of human psychology, human feelings (***The Dim***, 1917).

When painting ceased to represent real objects, it needed something to be composed of. While a traditional painting was "constructed" of recognizable forms (clouds, men, water, tables etc.), abstract art was looking for elements it could consist of. **Kazimir Malevich** (1878–1935) was the first to exhibit paintings composed of abstract geometrical elements. A simple geometrical form can give rise to numerous abstract forms. Thus a square when it is rotated forms first a cross and then a circle. A variety of figures can be composed of combinations of triangles. According to Malevich, compositions made of coloured, rhythmically arranged geometrical elements can give fullest expression to feeling. They can represent dynamics and statics, harmony and disharmony, flight and suspence.

Almost all avant-garde artists anticipated a new forthcoming era, a new stage in the history of the world which would change the conscience of man, so they tried to create a new art that would reflect the changed social, material and intellectual conditions of emerging modern life. This anticipation of changes in life prompted reforms in art. Malevich's work was addressed to future generations.

Until the mid-1910s his artistic career was very much like the careers of other painters involved in the search for innovative techniques. He was infatuated by Impressionism, Cézanne, Primitivism, Cubism and Futurism (**Portrait of Mikhail Matyushin**, 1913).

As a result of his reflections on the nature of art, its functions and aims, its history, he originated his own artistic and philosophical system, known as Suprematism. His **Black Suprematic Square** (1915) is a sort of its manifesto. The artist as if covers all the previous periods of art history with this black screen. He preserves the traditional form of a painting: black space (absence of colour) within the white frame (combination of all colours). Malevich's art was not an aesthetic reaction to reality, it rather expressed generalized ideas. He wrote: "Art is the feeling of reality without any images. A square is not an image, like a button or a socket is not electricity." The black square is as real as it is abstract, so it allows all sorts of interpretations.

For example, it may evoke historical associations. One of them is a legendary contest of artists held in ancient Greece. In accordance with its rules, it was won by the painter whose picture could not be distinguished from reality. A certain Parasias was announced the winner. His picture showed a black curtain and the public asked him to draw it aside to see the picture itself.

131. Lyubov Popova (1889–1924)
Architectonics of Painting. 1918
Oil on canvas. 62.2 x 44.5 cm

132. Kazimir Malevich (1878–1935)
Black Suprematic Square. 1915
Oil on canvas. 79.5 x 79.5 cm

133. Vladimir Tatlin (1885–1953)
Counter-Relief. 1914
Wood, metal and leather. 63 x 53 cm

While Malevich was called "a great prophet," **Vladimir Tatlin** (1885–1953) was called "a great craftsman." He attacked the seriousness of general ideas and took interest in materials. Tatlin strove to unify reality, form and techniques. His motto was "material, volume and construction." Material was his main means of expression and one of his major directives was "to construct" art. He believed that forms, paints and materials were of great artistic value, which he tried to demonstrate in his counter-reliefs, or painting reliefs (**Counter-Relief**, 1914). These samples of nonfigurative art seemed to intrude into reality. Tatlin admired modern industrial materials that had never been used in painting before. His work initiated the development of Constructivism.

A number of young artists under the guidance of Malevich enthusiastically began to create and develop modern art. These were **Alexander Rodchenko** (1891–1956), **Olga Rozanova** (1886–1918), **Ilya Chashnik** (1902–1929), **Ivan Klyun** (1873–1943), **Lyubov Popova** (1889–1924) and **El Lisitsky** (1890–1941). At the exhibition "Nonrepresentational Art and Suprematism" in 1919 they even rebuked Malevich for his works being not absolutely nonfigurative and having literary and philosophical aspects.

Some of them (Rodchenko, Popova and others) organized the First Working Group of Constructivists and devised their own theory of art. They thought that contemporary art was to improve the environment and to produce works, appropriate in the daily life of common people. Many of them became designers and worked at plants and factories. As a result of their activities there was formulated the ideology of Constructivism, one of major artistic movements in the 20th century. Born in Russia, Constructivist architecture spread to Europe and reached America.

Axonometric Painting (1920) by **Gustav Klutsis** (1895–1944) demonstrates the transformation of geometrical abstract art into Constructivism. The aesthetic principles of Constructivist painting were employed in many architectural designs.

134. Olga Rozanova (1886–1918)
Metronome. 1915
Oil on canvas. 46 x 33 cm

135. Ilya Chashnik (1902–1929)
Suprematism. 1923
Oil on canvas. 70.7 x 50 cm

136. Alexander Rodchenko (1891–1956)
Nonrepresentational Painting. Composition 56 (76).
The Plane Transformed by Its Textual Treatment. 1917
Oil on canvas. 88.5 x 70.5 cm

137. Ivan Klyun (1873–1943)
A Landscape Running by. 1915
Wood, metal, porcelain and wire. 77.5 x 61 cm

138. El Lisitsky (1890–1941)
New. Figurines. Stage-sets for the opera "Victory over the Sun"
(text by Alexei Kruchyonykh, music by Mikhail Matyushin). 1920–1921
Gouache, silver paint and lead pencil on paper. 49.5 x 37.9 cm

139. Gustav Klutsis (1895–1938)
Axonometric Painting. 1920
Oil on canvas. 96 x 57 cm

140. Yefim Cheptsov (1874–1951)
Meeting of a Village Party Organization. 1924
Oil on canvas. 57 x 77 cm

141. Konstantin Istomin (1887–1942)
University Students. 1933
Oil on canvas. 125.5 x 144.5 cm

Not all Russian artists of the period were involved in the pursuit of innovative forms and techniques. In the early 1920s there arose a protest against avant-garde experiments and renouncement of easel painting. Problems of narrative subjects began to be discussed again. At that moment the Association of Artists of Revolutionary Russia (AARR) was established which included many former members of the Society for Circulating Exhibitions dissolved in 1922. The declaration of the Association adopted in 1922 contained the following words: "Our duty to mankind is to create an artistic and documentary record of this greatest moment of history in its revolutionary surge forward... We are to express our artistic experience in the monumental forms of heroic realism." The declaration stated that art should be closely related to the struggle of the people for Socialism. It was to show the Red Army victories, the life of workers and peasants and to portray revolutionary leaders and heroes. This Socialist orientation led to the organization of regular exhibitions dealing with certain themes: "The Everyday Life of the Red Army," "The Everyday Life of Workers," "The Exposition Devoted to Vladimir Lenin" and others. For such exhibitions so-called "paintings in a grand style" were produced. This practice introduced by the AARR was current throughout the whole Soviet era. A "painting in a grand style" was a large-sized picture representing some ideological subject. Later it was called "a thematic painting." The AARR artists brought into use another important technical innovation: they often chose to portray their characters as if addressing the viewer. The *Meeting of a Village Party Organization* (1924) by **Yefim Cheptsov** (1874–1951) depicts real people from a Russian village. Such paintings in which the character was addressing the viewer were very popular. Demyan Bedny wrote a poem praising the picture as the hit of the AARR exhibition which represented common people sitting in a club and discussing their problems. Especially impressive was the figure of the orator speaking to his fellow villagers. He was probably not a phrase monger, but so dear and familiar to his listeners and viewers.

Even the former disciples of Constructivist painters attacked the creed of their teachers. They insisted on the significance of easel painting and thought it was necessary to inspire it with new ideas. The graduates of the Higher Art College, a higher educational establishment where Constructivism prevailed, organized the Society of Easel Painters. Art critics described their programme as the synthesis of early Russian icons with modern American art. Members of the Society looked for a new hero: "a man wearing a leather jacket," "Russian American," strong and efficient. They mostly chose urban subjects, as they believed that industrialization would launch the renovation of society. Another important subject of their oeuvre was sport which was also essential for the renovation, as a new man must be physically and mentally developed.

There were two major trends within the Society. One of them comprised those members who worked in a free "sketchy" manner and considered colour their main means of expression – **Alexander Labas** (1900–1983) and **Alexander Tyshler** (1898–1980). Members of the other trend – **Pyotr Williams** (1902–1947) and **Alexander Deyneka** (1899–1969) – worked in a decidedly delineatory style in which the brush was employed in the manner of a pen. Their contrasted planes and volumes painted with precise lines were to convey the rhythm and essence of the new epoch.

142. Pyotr Williams (1902–1947)
Portrait of Vsevolod Meyerhold. 1925
Oil on canvas. 230 x 180 cm

143. Alexander Labas (1900–1983)
Airship. 1931
Oil on canvas. 76 x 102 cm

All the artists of the Society made use of the method of assemblage, which distinguished their compositions from works of other groups. While in the oeuvre of Tyshler (***Sakko and Vanzetti***, 1927) this method had a metaphoric interpretation, Deyneka employed it for the clear, laconic expression of his ideas. He left nothing unsaid and his pictures had much in common with posters. Balancing Expressionism with Constructivism, Deyneka conveyed the fast tempo of modern life (***Construction of New Workshops***, 1926).

The highest professionalism, adherence to traditions and interest in the emotional aspect marked the work of "Four Arts" group that consisted of the artists who had never renounced the value of art forms (Lev Bruni (1894–1948) *Grove*, 1924; **Nikolay Kupreyanov** (1894–1933), ***Interior. "Good Night, Verochka!"***, 1924; Vladimir Lebedev (1891–1967), *A Nude with a Guitar*, 1929).

Many artists joined the group after the dissolution of "Makovets" whose artistic and philosophical programme had been influenced by the famous religious philosopher Pavel Florensky. The transcendent realm was most important for their worldview. They tried to create monumental forms conveying the ideas of Christian philosophy. One of them was Vasily Chekrygin (1897–1922).

Many of these artists did not betray their ideals in the period of Socialist Realism. ***University Students*** (1933) was painted by **Konstantin Istomin** (1887–1942), a successive member of "Makovets" and "Four Arts." The picture has a number of aspects. On the one hand, the theme of young people who would develop and build their country in future was popular in official art. On the other hand, Istomin's mastery and concern with aesthetic principles allowed him to avoid triviality and show his epoch in a lyrical vein. The painting reveals a dreamy, wistful mood and psychological profundity.

As it was in other totalitarian regimes, the Soviet government meant art to be an instrument of Communist ideology. It was supposed to serve the Socialist ideal and worldview. The only artistic method approved by the First

144. Antonina Sofronova (1892–1966)
Woman in Green. 1933
Oil on canvas. 69.8 x 55.5 cm

145. Nikolay Kupreyanov (1894–1933)
Interior. "Good Night, Verochka!" 1924
Indian ink on paper. 22.1 x 25.9 cm

146. Alexander Tyshler (1898–1980)
Sakko and Vanzetti. 1927
Oil on canvas. 81 x 62 cm

147. Tatyana Mavrina (1902–1996)
Portrait of Antonina Sofronova
with Her Daughter. 1938
Oil on canvas. 69.5 x 80.5 cm

148. Alexander Drevin (1889–1938)
Roe Deer. 1933
Oil on canvas. 67 x 82 cm

Congress of Writers was Socialist Realism. It was considered most appropriate for fulfilling the tasks given by the Soviets. In 1932 the Central Committee of the Communist Party issued a decree on the dissolution of all artistic groups and societies and the foundation of unions of artists, writers, composers etc., which made it much easier for the government to control cultural processes.

Nevertheless, various trends kept on competing with each other, whether it was manifest or not. The "Thirteen" group that had been officially dissolved, according to the above-mentioned decree, still adhered to the principles formulated by its members in the second half of the 1920s: they repudiated academic art, both old and new, and sought for modern art forms (**Tatyana Mavrina** (1902–1996), ***Portrait of Antonina Sofronova with Her Daughter***, 1938; Mikhail Sokolov (1885–1947), *Robespierre at the Platform*, 1932). Being skilful draughtsmen, they produced canvases which had the freshness and immediacy of sketches. **Alexander Drevin** (1889–1938) thought that the new was to be searched not in forms but human psychology. The quality of painting did not depend on its style. His pictures based on immediate impressions did not simply represent some phenomenon or event but acted as an emotional cathartic (***Roe Deer***, 1933).

149. Alexander Deyneka (1899–1969)
Construction of New Workshops. 1926
Oil on canvas. 209 x 200 cm

150. Yuri Pimenov (1903–1977)
New Moscow. 1937
Oil on canvas. 147 x 171 cm

151. Alexander Deyneka (1899–1969)
Future Pilots. 1938
Oil on canvas. 130 x 160 cm

152. Mikhail Nesterov (1862–1942)
Portrait of Vera Mukhina. 1940
Oil on canvas. 81 x 75 cm

153. Sarah Lebedeva (1892–1967)
Girl with a Butterfly. 1936
Bronze. Height 215 cm

154. Ivan Yefimov (1878–1959)
Dolphin. 1935
Copper; pedestal: glass and bronze.
Height 37 cm

155. Vera Mukhina (1889–1953)
The Worker and the Collective-Farmer
Model of the monument. 1936
Bronze. Height 160 cm

Though by the mid-1930s Socialist Realism was the only official style in Russian art, many works by mature as well as young artists revealed a high artistic quality and an independent attitude. They were more interested in art as form than in its social function (**Sarah Lebedeva** (1892–1967), *Girl with a Butterfly*, 1936; **Ivan Yefimov** (1878–1959), *Dolphin*, 1935).

Vera Mukhina (1889–1953) took lessons from the renowned French sculptor Emile-Antoine Bourdelle. Her most famous monumental piece *The Worker and the Collective-Farmer* (1937) was done in the so-called "grand" style of the 1930s. Mukhina succeeded in embodying the spirit of her epoch in it. She wrote that in previous periods sculpture had been used not only for decoration but expressed the ideals of its time. In 1937 the composition crowned the Soviet pavilion at the World Exhibition in Paris. The Tretyakov Gallery has the last version of the monument's model.

Many of Mukhina's works are based on the motif of two figures symbolizing unity and surge forward (*The Flame of the Revolution*, 1922–1923). The composition of the *Worker and the Collective-Farmer* consists of two figures that seem to be floating in the air. Mukhina said it was inspired by the "Nike of Samothrace." The visitors of the World Exhibition were astounded by the imposing sculptural group made of rust-proof steel and having the 34-metre pavilion as its pedestal. Romain Rolland wrote: "On the banks of the Seine two young giants rise their sickle and hammer towards the sky and we seem to hear them singing a heroic hymn calling the nations to freedom, unity and victory."

THE TRETYAKOV GALLERY

The majority of works displayed at the exhibitions of the 1930s – 1950s were done in the style of Socialist Realism. The essence of the method was the faithful representation of Socialist life which "the masses could understand and appreciate." In fact, the truthful representation was to show not the present-day reality but reality in its revolutionary development, the reality it must be in future. The task was rather abstract, yet the result had to be real.

The main genre was the so-called thematic picture. It combined elements of historical painting, landscape, portrait and everyday scene and was devoted to some ideologically important theme, such as the revolution, the Civil and Great Patriotic (World II) wars, struggle for peace and the building of Socialism. Socialist Realism used techniques of naturalistic idealization to portray positive heroes and Communist leaders (**Alexander Gerasimov** (1881–1963), ***Josef Stalin and Kliment Voroshilov in the Kremlin***, 1938). No flights of fancy or poetic aspirations were traceable in contemporary art.

156. Sergey Gerasimov (1885–1964)
Holiday in the Collective-Farm. 1937
Oil on canvas. 234 x 372 cm

157. Alexander Gerasimov (1881–1963)
Josef Stalin and Kliment Voroshilov in the Kremlin. 1938
Oil on canvas. 296 x 386 cm

158. Alexander Laktionov (1910–1972)
A Letter from the Front. 1947
Oil on canvas. 225 x 155 cm

THE TRETYAKOV GALLERY

It was almost impossible to arrive at a compromise. **Sergey Gerasimov** (1885–1964), a disciple of Konstantin Korovin, was a talented landscapist. In his ***Holiday in the Collective-Farm*** (1937) he used the techniques of plein air painting, particularly his favourite Impressionism, but they proved not to be in tune with his "political" task to represent the triumph of collectivization, to show a holiday of collective-farmers who had been working hard for the happy future of their native land. The poses of the characters are static, their faces immobile. They look unnatural against the background of a magnificent landscape bathed in the rays of the summer sun.

Only after World War II artists began to paint landscapes and genre scenes, along with thematic pictures. The aesthetics of Socialist Realism were in keeping with the convictions of **Arkady Plastov** (1893–1972). His pictures displayed the immediacy of sketches. He painted only what he loved and knew well. His characters are his fellow countrymen. His ***Hay-Making*** (1945) was executed in the first post-war summer. It expresses the joys of life in peace after the hard days of the war when the people have suffered so much and lost so many.

A Letter from the Front (1947) by **Alexander Laktionov** (1910–1972) became one of most famous genre paintings of its time. The artist has produced many copies of the picture for different museums. He wrote that his aim was to convey, in a heartfelt manner, the joy of the family who had received good news from the front. These people took close to heart everything that was going on at the front and rejoiced at the victories of the Soviet Army.

159. Arkady Plastov (1893–1972)
Hay-Making. 1945
Oil on canvas. 193 x 232 cm

160. Yury Zlotnikov (born 1930)
Shop Window. 1956. Oil on canvas. 113 x 147 cm

161. Vladimir Veysberg (1924–1985)
White Pitcher and a Plate on the Towel. 1960. Oil on canvas. 54 x 100 cm

162. Francisco Infante-Arana (born 1943)
Suprematic Games. 1968. Colour photographs; paper. 49.5 x 49.5 cm

163. Mikhail Shvartsman (1926–1997)
Trinitarian Space. 1981–1986. Tempera on canvas pasted on panel,
leukos (gesso white ground). 100 x 100 cm

164. Dmitry Plavinsky (born 1937)
Running in the Darkness. 1969. Etching on paper. 78.5 x 158 cm; 64.5 x 145.8 cm

THE TRETYAKOV GALLERY

All sorts of trends and styles existent in the first half of the 20th century were developed after 1945 (**Yury Zlotnikov** (born 1930), ***Shop Window***, 1956; **Dmitry Plavinsky** (born 1937), ***Running in the Darkness***, 1969; Oleg Kudryashov (born 1932), *The Last Work Produced in Moscow. Demons*, 1973). On the one hand, Socialist Realism was still the officially sponsored aesthetics, on the other hand, there appeared new, alternative, tendencies in the art of both "underground" painters and those who participated in official exhibitions.

The late 1950s – early 1960s were the years of the first "thaw," a period of relative liberalism, when it seemed that the Iron Curtain had ceased to exist. The historian Nikolay Eydelman wrote: "The mentality continued to be ideological but it had changed its essence. Yes we had a great idea and supported it. However the idea itself had changed. What 'they' had done was wrong, what 'we' were going to do now was right..."

As the identity of a work of art as a thing in itself was no longer rejected, artists turned to Impressionism. Instead of pompous large-sized pictures of the Stalin era, they attempted to accurately record visual reality and their own impressions (**Vladimir Veysberg** (1924–1985), ***White Pitcher and a Plate on the Towel***, 1960).

The "thaw" gave access to information. Representatives of unofficial art were first of all attracted by modern Western movements. Most of them were infatuated by abstract art which made it possible to get rid of the ideological and propagandistic functions of visual culture. It was later that they turned to the Russian avant-garde (**Francisco Infante-Arana** (born 1943), ***Suprematic Games***, 1968). Official art was oriented towards the traditions of the Renaissance, early Russian art and Cézanne.

165. Pavel Nikonov (born 1930)
Geologists. 1962
Oil on canvas. 185 x 225 cm

166. Nikolay Andronov (1929–1998)
Raftsmen. 1960–1961
Oil on canvas. 210 x 175 cm

167. Nina Zhilinskaya (1926–1995)
Family. 1968
Painted wood. Height 120 cm

These two trends differed in what they wanted to renovate in visual culture. Members of the official Union of Artists intended to renew Soviet art, while the artists who had been driven underground opposed to that art, and their opposition, ideological and stylistic, became the essence of unofficial art in the 1960s. One of the first underground groups was the Lianozovo Circle (named after a district on the outskirts of Moscow). Many artists from the Circle laid bare the darkness and fateful absurdity of everyday existence, in which people had to live in "communal" flats (a flat shared by several families) and barracks. The work of Oscar Rabin (born 1928) acquired philosophical aspect (*One Ruble Number Three*, 1967). Characteristic of him is the synthesis of the aesthetic principles of French art with the gloomy, sombre palette of the unofficial art of the 1930s. He added screened sand to paints which made the texture of his paintings rough and impressive.

The official art of the 1960s began to depict private family life, the tendency further developed in the 1970s. The choice of themes dealing with private life was one of most profound achievements of the artists of the 1960s. This can be illustrated by the sculptures of **Nina Zhilinskaya** (1926–1995) (*Family*, 1968) and **Adelaida Pologova** (born 1923) (*Go and Save My Path*, 1987). Most favourite material was wood that symbolized the simplicity of everyday existence with its joys, sorrows and duties. The sculptures, with their unfinished surface, looked as if cut out with an axe. The warm colour of wood produced a decorative effect. The sculpture of the period was to combine its intimate, lyrical character with new spatial contexts.

The exhibition dedicated to the 30th anniversary of the Moscow organization of Soviet artists (1962) became a turning point in the history of Soviet art. It included works of different groups, active in the period of the "thaw." But after the exhibition everything that did not follow the principles of Socialist Realism was severely criticized. *Geologists* (1962) by **Pavel Nikonov** (born 1930) provoked heated debates. The painting was unrealistic, non-narrative and metaphoric. It had nothing in common with Soviet poster-like pictures. These innovations appeared audacious, even provocative. The painting marked the end of the Severe (or Austere) style, a movement that had sought to endow images with a new integrity and strict verism, thereby overcoming the standards of official art of the Stalin era. The Severe style reached its acme in the years of the "thaw" (**Nikolay Andronov** (1929–1998), *Raftsmen* (1960–1961); **Oleg Komov** (1932–1994), *Glass*, 1958).

The Severe style was distinguished by a minimum of detail, a precise, rhythmical use of line and juxtaposition of colours and tones. This art was sincere and pathetic as the artists believed that society could be changed and improved.

The artists of the Moscow underground of the late 1950s – 1960s were interested in other, metaphoric, matters. Eager to determine the real nature of things and the sense of human existence, they dealt with these problems in religious and other aspects (Mikhail Shvartsman, Vladimir Veysberg and Dmitry Plavinsky).

Mikhail Shvartsman (1926–1997) devised his own, highly original, conception of art which he called "hieratism" (Greek "hieratikos," pagan priest). Employing the idiom of nonrepresentational art, he has evolved his own manner of painting that has no analogues in art history. He interprets abstract forms as symbols of spiritual phenomena. Compositions made of these forms have precise outlines. The forms are distributed on the canvas in an intricate manner, may interact with one another and as a result change their shape. In the ***Trinitarian Space*** (1981–1986) the forms seem to be drawn apart by the saturated white colour. Shvartsman uses the technique of superimposing different viewpoints, which gives rise to many space zones within which the forms are involved in a movement reflecting their transformation. The artist intends to illustrate the constant process of natural metamorphoses.

The painters of the metaphysical trend believed art to be a form of man's spiritual activity and did everything thoroughly for "great" art's sake. While the work of Shvartsman and Veysberg stayed far away from social reality, the most radical representatives of the underground dealt primarily with social matters.

168. Oleg Komov (1932–1994)
Glass. 1958
Bronze. Height 60 cm

169. Adelaida Pologova (born 1923)
Go and Save My Path. 1987
Painted and gilded wood. Height 150 cm

In the 1960s the official Moscow Union of Artists also sought for new forms, outside the above-mentioned Severe style. Some painters, like unofficial artists of the metaphysical trend, were inspired by the idea of creating "great" art. The oeuvre of **Victor Popkov** (1932–1974) with its metaphors, associations and lyrical tone was innovative for official art. The artist openly expressed his attitude to man and reality. He has developed a particular type of self-portrait which combines elements of different genres. The artist shows himself as a representative of his epoch reflecting on the fates and continuity of generations. In *My Father's Greatcoat* (1970–1972) he is depicted trying on his father's greatcoat. He "tells" the viewer about his time and himself "in the first person."

Popkov's works had a great impact on the aesthetic and artistic principles of younger painters, active in the 1970s. Then the Iron Curtain was established again, the artists were sealed off from contact with Western culture and turned to the aesthetics of the past. **Dmitry Zhilinsky** (born 1927) was the first to draw stylistically on the art of previous epochs and to superimpose its principles on the themes and methods of contemporary art. Zhilinsky, like Popkov, was also most influential among the generation of artists working in the late 1960s – early 1970s.

By the Sea. A Family (1962–1964) appeared when the Severe style was dominant in official art. Zhilinsky's manner, evocative of the Old Masters' paintings, lyrical tone and private themes contradicted the established Socialist pattern of the artists of the Severe style who showed the heroic working life of the Soviet people. Zhilinsky mostly portrayed in his pictures his family and friends.

The work of the young artists of the 1970s is lyrical in tone. Its themes are man and the outside world, the ego and the world, the painter's attitude to the world, the painter and his or her friends (**Irina Starzhenetskaya** (born 1943), *Two in a Boat*, 1982). The artists meditate on modern life; their interpretations, far from being simple, have psychological, emotional, intellectual and other aspects.

170. Victor Popkov (1932–1974)
My Father's Greatcoat. 1970–1972
Oil on canvas. 176 x 120 cm

171. Tatyana Nazarenko (born 1944)
Moscow Evening. 1978
Oil on canvas. 160 x 180 cm

172. Irina Starzhenetskaya (born 1943)
Two in a Boat. 1982
Oil on canvas. 113 x 137 cm

THE TRETYAKOV GALLERY

173. Dmitry Zhilinsky (born 1927)
By the Sea. A Family. 1962–1964
Tempera on masonite, lacquer
and leukos. 125 x 90 cm

174. Natalya Nesterova (born 1944)
Gogol's House. 1979
Oil on canvas. 160 x 160 cm

In that decade women-artists played a leading role in artistic life. Tatyana Nazarenko, Natalya Nesterova, Irina Starzhenetskaya, Olga Bulgakova and others had a hand in the development of new tendencies in the official Union of Artists circle.

The name of **Tatyana Nazarenko** (born 1944) was mentioned by art critics more often than others. As early as the 1970s she began to work in the idiom of Postmodernism, though the term itself was unknown either to Soviet artists or critics. ***Moscow Evening*** (1978) is highly representative of her early style. It displays the techniques she would use in her later works. Her paintings contain borrowed images, popular quotations and metaphors. They reveal the play of intellect and openly tell about the inner life of the artist.

Many painters of the 1970s focused on these aspects, that's why their art was described by critics as associative and metamorphic. Nazarenko confessed, they had to use allegories and metaphors in that period when everything was first allowed and then banned again.

In the 1970s the Primitive tradition revived in a new spirit (Neoprimitivism). One of its most illustrious exponents was **Natalya Nesterova** (born 1944). In Neoprimitivism she found her own means of expression and created individual interpretations of various subjects and phenomena. Her main theme was man's loneliness and isolation in the world (***Gogol's House***, 1979). Her paintings do not depict any action. They are staged in a puppet-theatre fashion where the characters always play the same parts. She combines the faithful, precise representation of details with the meditative, reflective mood of her pictures.

The first modern style to be allowed to official exhibitions was so-called Photorealism. Its aesthetic was formed in Western art in the 1970s. It portrays reality refracted through photographs. The painters of this trend work from photographs or slides, depicting them on canvas many times enlarged, in minute detail (Sergey Sherstyuk (1951–1998), *My Father and Me*, 1984). As a result reality is first reflected in photographs and then, through photographs, in painting.

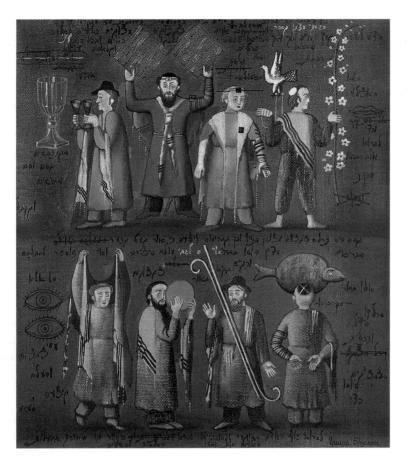

175. Grigory (Grisha) Bruskin (born 1945)
Alaphbet. Mid-1980s
Oil on canvas. 54 x 46 cm

176. Ilya Kabakov (born 1933)
Answers of the Experimental Group. 1970–1971
Enamel on masonite. 147 x 370 cm

177. Ivan Chuykov (born 1935)
Polyptych: Sea. 1990
Acrylic on masonite, photographs; collage. 172 x 254 cm

In Soviet time, when the artists were not satisfied with traditional styles, this art form was very popular. Photorealism made it possible to convey the pulsating rhythms of contemporary life. It mostly dealt with the themes of modern urban life (man and the technological revolution, man and nature) in their social and aesthetic aspects and tried to reconcile humanity with technology.

Conceptual and Sots art appeared in the late 1960s – early 1970s. These two trends differ from each other. Sots art employs and devalues myths of totalitarianism, political symbols, signs and clichés which were well-known to the people in the Soviet period and seriously influenced their attitudes. The artists of this trend often use the techniques of Pop art, even the name of their trend evokes associations with Pop art, but at the same time it denotes the difference between these two styles. The artists of Sots art are slyly ironic and their paintings have much in common with games (**Grigory Bruskin** (born 1945), **Alaphbet**, mid-1980s; **Ivan Chuykov** (born 1935), **Polyptych: Sea**, 1990).

Conceptual style prevails in the unofficial art of Moscow. It is often considered to be a Russian version of the Western Conceptual art of the late 1960s – early 1970s, so the term "Moscow Conceptualism" has been introduced. The movement was originated by **Ilya Kabakov** (born 1933). In the 1970s Conceptual art displayed accurate observation of social reality. Its major themes were ideology and political "mythology," social atmosphere and everyday life.

Conceptualists repudiate traditional values of art, particularly art as form. The aim of art is to express the painter's opinion of some important problem while the form of expression does not matter. The artists of the trend experiment with art as a language, its informative and communicative functions. They are interested in the correlation of a word and its visual image. Their works reveal a subtle interplay of visual and

Николай Борисович Миширов: Он хотел построить большой дом под Звенигородом.	**Аркадий Яковлевич Сипин:** Он всегда ходил очень медленно и что-нибудь объяснял на ходу.	**Лидия Аркадьевча Квасницкая:** Он был здесь.	**Иван Филимонович Михайлов:** Когда будешь ремонтировать сени, позови его.
Лина Звягинцева: Вечером ему несут еду.	**Анатолий Георгиевич Заревский:** К нему вела пустынная извилистая дорога.	**Лидия Кулькова:** Это могло быть только с ним.	**Бахран Ростанович Исламбеков:** Цветет он только летом.
Ефросинья Захаровна Кабачек: Если бы знать, что он...	**Арсф Баграмович Сукиасян:** Я впервые увидал его между деревьев с Картусского холма.	**Евдокия Климовна Пушкова:** И поставили его вон в тот угол комнаты.	**Мария Игнатьевна Яблонская:** Садитесь ближе к нему и согреетесь.
Матильда Ермоленко: Сестра хотела, чтобы он жил у нас.	**Лидия Самохвалова:** Он обычно приезжал на праздники.	**Иван Сидорович Кудрявцев:** Я съедал его целиком, немного поперчив.	**Сергей Анатольевич Похаржевский:** Вспомни, ты у него был с Леной и Александром Ильичем.
Софья Владимировна Беленькая: Мы вбинтили его согласно правилам, но он все равно падал.	**Анна Григорьевна Купельсон:** Мне кажется, что он не вернется никогда.	**Алексей Серебряный:** Здесь он оставил для тебя письмо.	**Володя Розенцвейг:** Может быть, он здесь?
Маша Колесова: Я ждала его в саду на углу Сретенки.	**Аркадий Дмитриевич Непейвода:** Я вчера его видел на улице.	**Анатолий Косоланов:** Вместе с Марихой он ходил в далекий лес.	**Маргарита Робинсон:** Вечером он ушел один.
Гораций Велениинович Востоков: Он подплывает тихо к берегу и останавливается.	**Леонид Стахиевич Введенский:** Вечером, при закате он почти не виден.	**Софья Никитична Шиворотова:** Покрасим его в ярко зеленый цвет.	**Рабик Мисропян:** Он живет за той горой?
Владик Шаповалов: Под ним было тепло и тихо.	**Александр Непомнящий:** Я отодвинул камень, стал на колени и заглянул в него.	**Марк Антонович Городовик:** Он привозил Власовым свежий хлеб, молоко и фрукты.	**Анечка Пустовойт:** Можно мне пойти к нему?
Зинаида Михайловна Шаховская: Он прячется под листьями и тихо спит.	**Надежда Леонидовна Покровская:** Ты напрасно сруби его.	**Любовь Петровна Молоканова:** Когда он окончился, то все было покрыто битым кирпичом, обедками и обрывками обои.	**Алексей Дмитриевич Лисицын:** Он четвертый, если считать от угла.

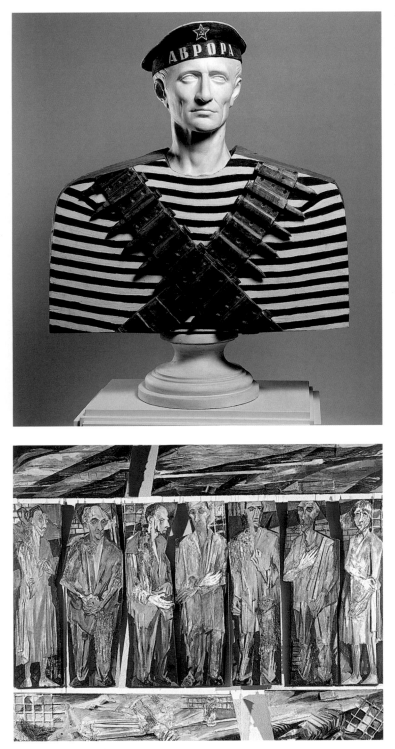

verbal elements, and sometimes the latter forces out the former (Ilya Kabakov (born 1933), ***Answers of the Experimental Group***, 1970–1971).

A new generation of artists that started their careers in the 1980s appreciated art as form (Lev Tabenkin (born 1952), *On the Way*, 1991). In reaction to the eclectic borrowed images of Postmodernism, they chose a single traditional style to work in. **Maxim Kantor** (born 1957) adopts not only some elements of Expressionism but all its principles and techniques. He is interested in social themes and treats them without irony. In the polyptych ***Chernobyl. The Star "Wormwood"*** (1986–1987) the artist turns to more general problems than the accident at the Chernobyl nuclear power station. The second part of the picture's name is taken from the Revelation of St John: "A great star blazing like a torch, fell from the sky on a third of the rivers and on the springs of water – the name of the star is Wormwood (Bitterness). And a third of the waters turned bitter and many people died" (Rev. 8:10,11) (Slavonic "chernobyl" means "wormwood"). Concluding from the particular to the general, the artist interprets the tragic accident at Chernobyl as the end of the world and portrays members of his family there, as if personalizing the event, which is characteristic of the artworks from the 1960s – 1970s.

The exhibition is completed by the works of Moscow Conceptual artists from the late 1970s – 1980s. Conceptual art does not recognize traditional aesthetic principles. It has opened the way to activities notable for their defiance of conventional expectations. It imposes art on reality and eliminates distinctions between them (**Igor Makarevich** (born 1943), Photoinstallation: ***Changes***, 1978).

In the 1980s the most popular form of Conceptual art was "performance art" or "happenings." The public was specially invited to them. This form employs techniques akin to these used in theatre, the artists themselves become a kind of media. Thus they endeavour to extend the boundaries of expression. A piece of art ceases to be a material object and turns into the creative process. The performance artists try to represent in simple and laconic actions the projects that can't be realized in art. They acclaim the creative process as having a high value, irrespective of its aesthetic and artistic result.

It is impossible to name all the styles and artists displayed in the Tretyakov Gallery building on Krymsky Val. Here Russian art is not divided into the pre-Soviet, Soviet and post-Soviet epochs but is shown as a whole. Nevertheless it comprises many styles, trends and movements that are not of equal social, artistic and aesthetic quality. This grandiose retrospective covers not only the history of art but the history of Russia itself. In spite of the fact that the 20th century was a hard and complicated period for Russia, many artists and paintings from the time enjoy great renown.

178. Boris Orlov (born 1941)
Emperor. 1975
Enamel on wood and plaster. Height 85 cm

179. Maxim Kantor (born 1957)
Chernobyl. The Star "Wormwood." 1986–1987
Polyptych consisting of 11 parts
Oil and tempera on wood and plaster, leukos

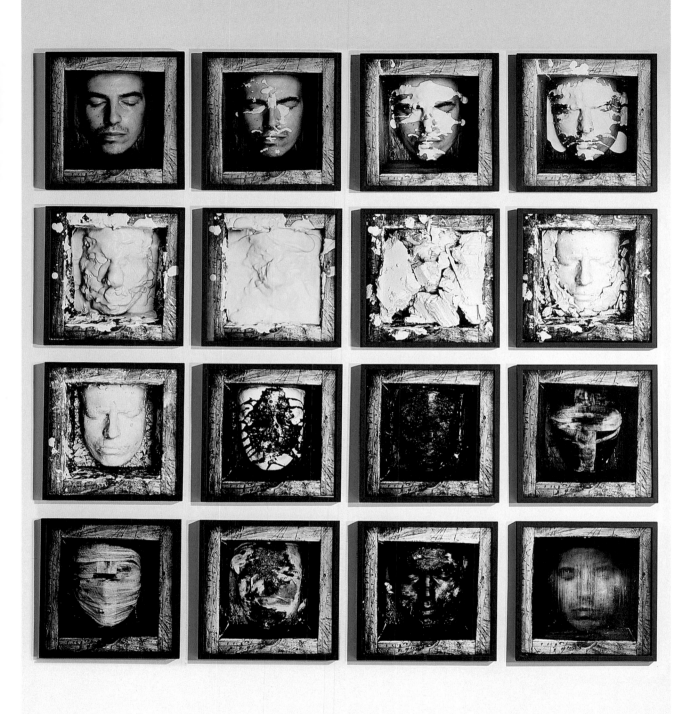

180. Igor Makarevich (born 1943)
Photoinstallation: ***Changes***. 1978
Black-and-white photographs, photographic paper.
Parts 1–16, each 50 x 50 cm

Museum Church of St Nicholas in Tolmachi

Church of St Nicholas in Tolmachi was first mentioned in documents in the 17th century. Since the mid-19th century its history has been connected with the family of Pavel Tretyakov who regularly attended services here and was its generous benefactor. There is a plaque commemorating him inside the building. In 1929 the church was closed and transferred to the control of the State Tretyakov Gallery. In 1997 it was restored. Now it looks exactly like it did in Tretyakov's lifetime, after being redesigned by the architect Fyodor Shestakov in 1833–1858. Noteworthy in the interior are 19th-century murals showing Old and New Testament subjects painted in the academic manner and the icons from the gallery stocks (12th–19th centuries).

The highlight of the church interior is the five-tiered iconostasis dating from the 17th century. It contains, to the right of the royal doors, the **icon of St Nicholas of Myra** (early 17th century) to whom the church is dedicated. In front of the iconostasis, placed in a special case, is the **Vladimir icon of the Mother of God** (1100–1130s), one of the most venerated icons in Russia.

In 1992 services were resumed in the church that received status of the gallery church and at the same time became one of its research departments, so it is opened both for gallery visitors and churchgoers.

Interior of the Museum Church of St Nicholas in Tolmachi. Iconostasis

Icon of St Nicholas. Early 17th century. Moscow
Tempera on panel, leukos. 145 x 105.5 cm

House-Museum of Pavel Korin

Pavel Korin (1892–1967) started his career as an icon painter. He worked for the Monastery of the Don Icon of the Mother of God and Sts Martha and Mary's Convent.

In 1933 Korin, then a renowned painter, with the assistance of Maxim Gorky, got a workshop of his own in Malaya Pirogovskaya Street 16. In 1971 his memorial museum was opened on its premises. It features many works by the famous artist which have not been exhibited until lately. These are sketches for the expressive and tragic portraits (1929–1937) from Korin's unrealized monumental painting *Farewell to Rus. Requiem*. The artist had to suspend his work on the canvas when a new campaign of political terror was launched by Stalin. The museum also houses sketches for the mosaics decorating the "Komsomolskaya-Koltsevaya" metro station for which Korin was awarded the State Prize in 1952.

On view are photographs and documents illustrating his work as a restorer. Together with his brother Alexander, Korin restored paintings from the Dresden Gallery.

Korin was a connoisseur of early Russian art. On display is a superb collection of 12th – 19th-century icons which includes fine specimens of the Stroganov school, icons painted in the village of Palekh and family icons of the Korins as well as early Russian figurines and 16th-century embroidery.

Interior of Pavel Korin's workshop. Near the wall are sketches for the unrealized painting *Farewell to Rus. Requiem*.

Russian icons and objects of decorative art collected by Pavel Korin.

Memorial Studio of the Sculptor Anna Golubkina

Anna Golubkina (1864–1927) was one of most talented and illustrious sculptors of the 20th century. Born of a family of peasants, she worked hard to become a professional sculptor. She started her education in Moscow, then was taught by the leading masters of St Petersburg and Paris where she enjoyed advice of Auguste Rodin.

One of her celebrated works is the monumental relief *Swimmer* (*Wave*, *The Sea of Life*, 1901), commissioned by Savva Mamontov, which is set up above the entrance of the Moscow Arts Theatre in Kamergersky Lane.

Golubkina has produced a series of expressive sculptural portraits which reveal psychological profundity. She employs a variety of techniques to convey her sitter's character and temperament. Most noteworthy are the portraits of the art patron Savva Mamontov, the famous Symbolist writer Andrey Bely and the leading Symbolist poet Vyacheslav Ivanov.

Since 1910 Golubkina lived in a flat adjacent to her studio in Bolshoy Levshinsky Lane 12. In 1932 her museum was opened there. It holds her private belongings and instruments, sculptures, cameos and sketches.

Interior of the studio

House-Museum of Victor Vasnetsov

Victor Vasnetsov (1848–1926) was inspired by Russian history, old traditions, early Russian art and Moscow's traditional lifestyle. He appreciated early Russian architecture and employed its motifs in the designs of the fairy-tale "hut on a hen's legs" (1883) in the Mamontov estate in Abramtsevo, his own log "terem" house (1894, now in Vasnetsov Lane 13), the house of the famous art collector Ivan Tsvetkov on the Prechistenskaya Embankment (1901–1903) and the facade of the Tretyakov Gallery (1900–1905) in Lavrushinsky Lane.

Many famous people visited his house: Maxim Gorky, Anton Chekhov, Vladimir Gilyarovsky, Fyodor Chaliapin, Pavel Tretyakov, Savva Mamontov, Isaac Levitan, Mikhail Nesterov, Valentin Serov, Vasily Surikov, Ilya Repin, Vasily Polenov and others. The hallmarks of the museum are the stoves designed by Vasnetsov and covered with the tiles made after Mikhail Vrubel's sketches, furniture in Neo-Russian style, a collection of arms, Vasnetsov's graphic works and architectural designs.

House-Museum of Victor Vasnetsov. General view

Memorial Flat of Apollinary Vasnetsov

Apollinary Vasnetsov (1856–1933) shared his brother's love for old Russian culture. He is renowned for his historical townscapes in which he portrayed in minute detail Moscow's streets, squares and architectural ensembles as they looked in the Middle Ages.

Vasnetsov's rich imagination and extensive knowledge of Moscow's history and archaeology allowed him to "reconstruct" mediaeval views of the city. He thoroughly studied old maps, plans, engravings and miniatures showing ancient architecture, objects of everyday life and old wooden structures. In 1918–1928 he directed the Committee for the Research of Old Moscow and supervised archaeological excavations in the city centre. His celebrated album of lithographs "Ancient Moscow" and a series of picturesque and precise watercolour topographical views of 12th – 19th-century Moscow reveal his talent of an artist and his erudition of a scholar.

Since 1904 Vasnetsov lived in Furmanny Lane 6, his museum was opened there in 1965. The exhibition includes works by Vasnetsov, furniture made after his design, his personal belongings and documents illustrating his scholastic activities.

Vasnetsov's workshop. On the wall is the canvas *Winter Sleep (Winter)* from the *Seasons* series. 1908–1914. Oil on canvas. 122 x 177 cm

Vasnetsov's workshop with his picture *The Murmur of the Old Park* on the easel. 1926. Oil on canvas. 106 x 176.5 cm
In the centre of the wall is *Iphigeneia in Tauris*. 1889–1924
Oil on canvas. 78 x 145 cm